Helen W. Boyden

Boyden's Speaker

For Primary Grades

Helen W. Boyden

Boyden's Speaker
For Primary Grades

ISBN/EAN: 9783337779344

Printed in Europe, USA, Canada, Australia, Japan

Cover: Foto ©Thomas Meinert / pixelio.de

More available books at **www.hansebooks.com**

BOYDEN'S SPEAKER.

FOR PRIMARY GRADES.

EDITED AND COMPILED

BY

HELEN W. BOYDEN,

AUTHOR OF STUDENTS' FIRST READER, BOYDEN'S SUPPLEMENTARY READER.

CHICAGO:

GEO. SHERWOOD & CO.

1890.

PREFACE.

SUGGESTIONS FOR INEXPERIENCED TEACHERS.

> "Be not weary or downcast;
> Patience holds the gate at last."

When copying a piece underline the emphasized words and inform the child why you have done so. Read the selection to the pupil, having him repeat it after you, before he commits it to memory.

Use tact in assigning pieces; study the fitness as well as the capability of the child, forgetting not the season, the occasion, etc. The pupil who speaks rhyme in a sing-song tone, may render prose well. Short, sensible sentiments enable overgrown children to appear creditably. Timid ones gain courage when standing in groups; each pupil reciting one stanza. Sensible children, with clear voices and self-confidence, are required for dialogues. Special dressing is not absolutely necessary, yet it is very desirable.

Do not attempt too much in concert recitations, teach slowly and well, keep up the interest, always try to use the same emphasis, inflections, tones, etc., that you did when you first read the poem to the school. Such pieces are excellent for exhibition days and opening exercises, aside from the pleasure and profit that the children have derived from them.

Group all recitations, on the programme, topically, and teach songs that will harmonize with them.

Decorate the walls with flags and boughs, the blackboards with proverbs, and short sentiments, but do not overdo the matter. Let the harmonious, symmetrical appearance of your decorations not only refresh and rest the eyes of visitors, but also be a lesson in good taste to your pupils; in other words, if you decorate, *decorate.*

Chicago, 1890.   *H. W. B.*

CONTENTS.

6 CONTENTS.

10 CONTENTS.

BOYDEN'S SPEAKER.

SELECTIONS FOR THE BLACKBOARD.

Golden Rule.—Do unto others as you would have them do unto you.

Think of ease, but work.—*Poor Richard.*

Peace on earth, good will to men.

Poor freedom is better than rich slavery.

Truth is strong.

A good name will shine forever.

Keep to the truth.

Love your country.

Step by step one goes a long way.

> Do well the duty of a child,
> And manhood's task is well begun.
>
> —*Burleigh.*
>
> Who sows a field or trains a flower,
> Or plants a tree, is more than all.
>
> —*Whittier.*

Freedom forever.

Always have time to do good.

Be good, and love to do good.—*Alcott.*

He that does good to another man, does also good to himself.—*Seneca.*

It is no true alms the hand can hold.—*Lowell.*

> Not at a bound,
> But round on round,
> Up the ladder we're climbing.

We will die, if we cannot live free men.—*Josiah Quincy, Jr.*

Time lost can never be regained.

One to-day is worth two to-morrows.—*Poor Richard.*

Take care of the minutes; the hours will take care of themselves.

A time for everything and everything in its time.

> Our to-days and yesterdays
> Are the blocks with which we build.
>> —*Longfellow.*

> The mighty West shall bless the East,
>> And sea shall answer sea,
> And mountain unto mountain call,
>> PRAISE GOD, FOR WE ARE FREE!
>>> *Whittier.*

WHAT BELL AND GUN TELL.

> Even now, the peal of bell and gun,
>> And hills aflame,
> Tell of the first great triumph won
>> In Freedom's name.

> The long night dies; the welcome gray
>> Of dawn we see;
> Speed up the heavens thy perfect day,
>> God of the free!
>>> —*Whittier.*

OUR FLAG.

> Its hues are all of heaven—
> The red of sunset's dye,
> The whiteness of the moon-lit cloud,
> The blue of morning's sky.
>> —*Whittier.*

UNION.

> Union! That word hath shone on high
> In starry letters to the sky—
> It is our country's name.   —*Dr. Cummings.*

UNITY.

One flag, one land, one heart, one hand,
One Nation, evermore!

—*O. W. Holmes.*

INDEPENDENCE DAY.

The United States is the only country with a known birth-day. All the rest began they knew not when, and grew into power they knew not how.

If there had been no Independence day, England and America would not be as great as each actually is. There is no "Republican," no "Democrat," on the Fourth of July—all are Americans.

All feel that their country is greater than party.

CENTENNIAL HYMN.

First Child—

Our father's God! from out whose hand
The centuries fall like grains of sand,
We meet to-day, united, free,
And loyal to our land and Thee,
To thank Thee for the era done,
And trust Thee for the opening one.

*　　*　　*　　*

Second Child—

O, make Thou us, through centuries long,
In peace secure, in justice strong;
Around our gift of freedom draw
The safeguards of thy righteous law;
And, cast in some diviner mold,
Let the new cycle shame the old.

—*Whittier.*

OUR COUNTRY.

Her eagle wing shall Victory wave
Around the arm that strikes to save;
And Earth, applauding, see

The friend of every friendless name,
Foremost in bliss and strength and fame,
The Friend of Freedom, *free !*

—*Christian Observer.*

PATRIOTIC ADVICE.

Stand by our flag to-day—
Keep to the Union true—
Under our flag, while yet we may
Hurrah for the red, white, and blue.

(*Waves a flag.*)

OUR COUNTRY.

There is no other land like thee,
No dearer shore;
Thou art the shelter of the free;
The home, the port of liberty,
Thou hast been and ever shall be,
Till time is o'er.

—*Percival.*

THE FLAG.

Our flag on the land and our flag on the ocean,
An angel of peace wheresoever it goes,
Nobly sustained by Columbia's devotion,
The angel of death it shall be to our foes!

—*T. Buchanan Read.*

THE AMERICAN FLAG.

When Freedom from her mountain height,
Unfurled her standard to the air,
She tore the azure robe of night,
And set the stars of glory there!
She mingled with its gorgeous dyes
The milky baldric of the skies,
And striped its pure celestial white
With streakings of the morning light.

—*Jos. Rodman Drake.*

LITTLE BOY'S SPEECH.

The noblest thing, next to God, that a man can love, is country.—*Beecher.*

ONE.

LIBERTY *and* UNION, *now and forever*, ONE AND INSEPAR-ABLE.—*Webster.*

OUR STARRY FLAG.

It is the rainbow in the morning sky,
The bow that to the tempest owes its birth;
A shield, a refuge, and a promise high,
To all the oppressed of earth.

The talisman of all the trodden down,
A heavenly sign upon the cloud inwrought,
In token that no deluge more shall drown
The world of human thought.

Youth's Companion.   —*G. H. C.*

UNFURLING THE FLAG.

First Child—
Spread her broad banner to storm and to sun;
Heaven keep her ever free,
Wide as o'er land and sea
Floats the fair emblem her heroes have won!
—*O. W. Holmes.*

Second Child—
Newly bright thro' the glistening light,
The flag went grandly sweeping,
Gleaming and bold were its braids of gold,
And flashed in the sun-ray's kissing;
Red, white, and blue, were of deepest hue—
And none of the stars were missing.
—*Will Carleton.*

OUR BANNER.

That flag is known on every shore
The standard of a gallant band,

Alike unstained in peace or war,
It floats o'erFreedom's happy land.

UP WITH OUR BANNER.

Up with our banner bright,
Sprinkled with starry light,
Spread its fair emblems from mountain to shore,
While through the sounding sky
Loud rings the Nation's cry,—
UNION AND LIBERTY! ONE EVERMORE!

—O. W. Holmes.

IN PEACE.

How shall I serve my father's land?
There are no battles to be won,
No deeds that heroes might have done,
No lives to give at her command.

Nay, none of these;—but lives to live,
Within of gentle soul and pure,
Without of zeal and courage, sure,
For all the best that life can give.

And then, to crown the finished span,
To honor, country and her dead,
'Twere meet enough that it be said:
"He lived a true American."

Youth's Companion.   *M. A. D. W. Howe. Jr.*

FLOWER OF LIBERTY.

First Child—

What flower is this that greets the morn,
Its hues from Heaven so freshly born!
With burning star and flaming band
It kindles all the sunset land:
O, tell us what its name may be,—
Is this the Flower of Liberty?

Second Child—

> It is the banner of the free,
> The starry Flower of Liberty!

Third Child—

> Behold its streaming rays unite,
> One mingled flood of braided light,—
> The red that fires the Southern rose,
> With spotless white from Northern snows,
> And, spangled o'er its azure, see
> The sister stars of Liberty!

School—

> Then hail the banner of the free,
> The starry Flower of Liberty!

Fourth Child—

> Thy sacred leaves, fair Freedom's flower,
> Shall ever float on dome and tower,
> To all their heavenly colors true,
> In blackening frost or crimson dew,— .
> And God love us as we love thee,
> Thrice holy Flower of Liberty!

School—

> Then hail the banner of the free,
> The starry Flower of Liberty!
>
> *—O. W. Holmes.*

THE AMERICAN FLAG.

[Provide each Pupil with a flag.]

First Pupil—

> This is our flag, and may it wave
> Wide over land and sea!
> Tho' others love a different flag,
> This is the flag for me.

School, or pupils that are speaking—

> And that's the flag for all our land
> We will revere no other,
> And he who loves the symbol fair,
> Shall be to us a brother.

Second Pupil—

> America's the land we love,
> Our broad, fair land so free,
> And, schoolmates, whereso'er I go,
> This is the flag for me.

School—

> And that's the flag for me, etc.

Third Pupil—

> These glorious stars and radiant stripes
> With youthful joy I see;
> May no rude hand its beauty mar,
> This is the flag for me.

School—

> And that's the flag for me, etc.

THE WORDS OF LINCOLN.

This Nation under God shall have a new birth of freedom, and that government of the people, by the people, for the people, shall not perish from the earth.—*Abraham Lincoln.*

ONE FLAG ARE WE.

> Creed nor faction can divide us,
> Race nor language can divide us,
> Still, whatever fate betide us,
> Children of the flag are we.
>
> —*Chas. Halpine.*

A STATESMAN'S WORDS.

Let our object be our country, our whole country and nothing but our country. And by the blessing of God, may that country itself become a vast and splendid monument, not of oppression and terror, but of wisdom, of peace, and of liberty, upon which the world may gaze with admiration forever.—*Daniel Webster.*

HURRAH FOR FREEDOM'S FLAG.

"Then, hurrah, hurrah, for Freedom's flag!
We hail with ringing cheers,
Its glowing bars and clustering stars,
That have braved a hundred years."

OUR FLAG.

Forever float that standard sheet,
Where breathes the foe but falls before us,
With Freedom's soil beneath our feet,
And Freedom's banner streaming o'er us.
—*Drake.*

EMPIRE OF THE FREE.

And thou, O, Empire of the free!
Beloved land, God compass thee!

Still keep and guard thee in thy ways,
Still prosper thee in coming days!

And ye, O, People brave and blest!
Love still your country's cause the best;

Uphold her faith, maintain her powers,
Defend her ramparts and her towers.
—*Henry M. Look.*

OUR SENTIMENTS.

First small boy—

The union of hearts, the union of hands, and the flag of
the Union forever.—*G. P. Morris.*

Second small boy—

We crave no land beside, whatever may betide
The great Republic—God ever bless and guide.
Amen.

OUR FLAG.

The patriot Wendóver of old,
Suggested for our starry fold
    (The standard of the free)
Alternate stripes of white and red
In a blue field like that o'er head,
    To float o'er land and sea.

He saw the soft stars shining through
The radiant realm of azure hue,
    A hint by nature given
To statesmen true and brave and wise,
And copied from the glowing skies
    The flag he saw in heaven.

Our fathers looked to heaven on high,
And transcribed from the starlit sky
    The beautiful design;
The blue, sprinkled with points of light,
To lead us in the path aright,
    Where lamps immortal shine.

The flag that waves from spire and mast,
Though baptized in the battle blast,
    May fly without surcease
A light upon the land and sea,
A promise and a prophesy
    Of centuries of peace.

                   —*George H. Boker.*

THE OLD BATTLE SHIP.

But three feet good of that old wood,
    So scarred in war and rotten,
Was thrown aside, unknown its pride,
    Its honors all forgotten.

When as in shade the block was laid,
    Two robins perching on it,
Thought that place best to build a nest—
    They planned it, and have done it.

The splintered spot which lodged a shot,
　　Is lined with moss and feather,
And chirping loud, a callow brood
　　Are nestling up together.

How full of bliss—how peaceful is
　　That spot the soft nest caging,
Where war's alarms and blood-stained arms
　　Were once around it raging.
　　　　　　　　　　　—Tupper.

THE SHIP OF STATE.

Thou, too, sail on, O, ship of State!
Sail on, O, UNION, strong and great!
Humanity with all its fears,
With all its hopes of future years,
Is hanging breathless on thy fate!
We know what master laid thy keel,
What workman wrought thy ribs of steel,
Who made each mast, and sail, and rope,
What anvils rang, what hammers beat,
In what a forge and what a heat
Were shaped the anchors of thy hope!
Fear not each sudden sound and shock,
'Tis of the wave and not the rock;
'Tis but the flapping of the sail,
And not a rent made by the gale!
In spite of rock and tempest's roar,
In spite of false lights on the shore,
Sail on, nor fear to breast the sea!
Our hearts, our hopes, are all with thee,
Our hearts, our hopes, our prayers, our tears,
Our faith triumphant o'er our fears,
Are all with thee,—are all with thee!
　　　　　—Henry Wadsworth Longfellow.

THE STRUGGLE'S O'ER.

Thank God, the struggle's over, peace reigns in all our land,
United now as brothers, forever let us stand:
One flag, one country—union—no North, South, East or West,

Each trying with the other to do the very best;
With millions of defenders to rally at its call,
Old Glory is an emblem that truthful speaks to all;
We love to look upon it as it proudly floats for aye,
No star is darkly blotted, no stripe but of royal dye.

—B. Readwalls.

THE SONG OF SHERMAN'S ARMY.

A pillar of fire by night,
A pillar of smoke by day,
Some hours of march—then a halt to fight.
And so we hold our way;
Some hours of march—then a halt to fight,
As on we hold our way.

Over mountain and plain and stream,
To some bright Atlantic bay,
With our arms aflash in the morning beam,
We hold our festal way;
With our arms aflash in the morning beam,
We hold our checkless way!

There is terror wherever we come;
There is terror and wild dismay
When they see the Old Flag and hear the drum
Announce us on the way;
When they see the Old Flag and hear the drum
Beating time to our onward way.

—Charles G. Halpine.

THE FLAG.

Oh, the flag of our own country,
Let it wave on high:
May the stars and stripes ne'er perish
And no foe come nigh.

May we ever love its colors,
Red and white and blue:
May we one and all prove faithful,
Faithful, kind and true.

—Sylvia Manning.

WORDS OF EMINENT MEN.

First Child—

Human happiness has no perfect security but freedom;— freedom none but virtue;— virtue none but knowledge.

—Quincy.

Second Child—

I know not what course others may take, but, as for me, give me liberty or give me *death!—Patrick Henry*

Third Child—

In defense of our civil and religious rights, we dare oppose the world; with the God of armies on our side, even the God who fought our father's battles, we fear not the hour of trial.

—Josiah Quincy, Jr.

PEACE PROCLAIMS.

Peace proclaims on sea and shore,
One Country now and evermore!

—O. W. Holmes.

GARFIELD'S WORDS.

Heroes did not make our liberties, they but reflected and illustrated them.—*James A. Garfield.*

OUR SENTIMENTS ABOUT THE FLAG.

A boy, with a large flag in his hand, steps forward and says:—

Boys, here is our flag; what have you to say for it?

Second Boy—

The citizen of the United States who loves any flag better than this one is a traitor.—*D. R. Breed.*

Third Boy—

We join ourselves to no party that does not carry the flag and keep step to the music of the Union.—*Rufus Choate.*

Fourth Boy—
It is the duty of every American citizen to rally around the flag of his country.—*Stephen A. Douglas.*

Fifth Boy—
I will never desert the flag of my country and the glory of its truth.—*James A. Garfield.*

Sixth Boy—
Patriotism is not the mere holding of a great flag unfurled, but making it the goodliest flag in the world.—*Linton.*

School sing—
"AMERICA, OUR FLAG, OUR HOME."—*Auntie Em's Song Leaves.*

TRUE PATRIOTISM.

There are two kinds of patriotism—two species of love of country. There is that blind idolatry a man feels for the land of his birth simply because it is his native land. It is a feeling that is born at the fireside, and clusters around the homestead. It is nourished by the traditions of the past, and by the memories of the hallowed dead. It burns in the heart, it flows through the veins, and vibrates through the entire nervous system. It is a noble sentiment. But there is also another kind of patriotism—a patriotism which has its birth in the brain center, nourished by reason and thought. It is as steadfast in the heart of the man who comes to America, making it the land of his choice, as in the heart of him who is to the manor born.—*Carter H. Harrison.*

"WHO DARES?"

" Who dares? " this was the patriot's cry,
As striding from the desk he came,
" Come out with me in Freedom's name,
For her to live, for her to die? "
A hundred hands flung up reply,
A hundred voices answered, " I!"
—*Thomas Buchanan Read.*

LOVE OF COUNTRY.

There is deep down in the hearts of the American people a strong and abiding love of our country which no surface storms of passion can ever shake.—*James A. Garfield.*

FOR OUR COUNTRY.

First Child—
> Through glade and glen, from deep to deep,
> The silent host of heroes sleep—

> Their arms at rest, their labor done,
> The battle fought, the vict'ry won.

Second Child—
> O'er some, through all the golden day,
> Fame's loudest echoes grandly play,

> And immortelle and myrtle weave
> A dewy wreath for them at eve,

> While floats around them, low and sweet,
> The prayer which loving lips repeat.

Third Child—
> O'er many more no trophies rise—
> Unnamed, unknown each sleeper lies,

> With wilding fern or asphodel
> Alone to mark where valor fell.

Fourth Child—
> What though above their dreamless sleep
> No mourner's head be bowed to weep?

> What though no sage their record write,
> Nor grateful bard their fame indite?

Fifth Child—
> Their glory gleams o'er every plain
> That bears their blood's redeeming stain:

> Like the soft splendor of the stars
> When first they break their twilight bars.
>   —*Henry M. Look.*

SLEEP, SONS OF FREEDOM.

Sleep, ye sons of Freedom, sleep,
    Where bugles never sound;
Nor clash of steel, nor cannon's boom,
    Disturb your rest profound!
The glorious flag of fadeless hues,
    'Neath which ye fought and fell,
Shall ever proudly wave on high,
    And of your valor tell.

                      —*J. W. Cathcart.*

MEMORIAL DAY.

Procession of children with flowers pass in front of the two speakers and into the dressing room; as they pass, the smaller speaker says:—

Where are all of those children going with their arms full of flowers?

Large Boy—

To the cemetery to strew the flowers on the soldiers' graves.

Small Boy—

And why should they lay them on the soldiers'. graves; a dead man knows not what they do, neither can he see the pretty blossoms, and they will only wither and die.

Large Boy—

That is very true; but by that remembrance of the noble deeds of the fallen heroes we inspire the living to be

    "True to the flag on the field and the wave,
      Living to honor it, dying to save."

Small Boy—

Will only the children decorate the graves?

Large Boy—

O, no! All that wish may do it. Many a hero will lay a flag and a flower on a comrade's grave.

Small Boy—

Why did they fight: is it not wicked?

Large Boy—

They fought for freedom and justice. It is always right to defend one's country by fighting when all other means have failed.

Small Boy (raising his hand)—

Listen!

Children, with flowers, sing softly—

(TUNE: "The Vacant Chair.")

> On the graves of all our heroes
> Lay we flowers of every hue,
> As an off'ring of remembrance—
> Laurels for the brave and true.

—*Helen W. Boyden.*

PEACE SHALL UNITE.

> Peace shall unite us again and forever
> Tho' thousands lie cold in the graves of the wars;
> Those who survive them shall never prove, never,
> False to the flag of the stripes and stars!

—*Geo. H. Boker.*

THE "MISSING" IN THE WILDERNESS.

> But Nature knows no wilderness;
> There are no "missing" in her numbered ways.
> In her great heart is no forgetfulness.
> Each grave she keeps she will adorn, caress,
> We cannot lay such wreaths as Summer lays,
> And all her days are Decoration Days!

—*H. H.*

AMERICA'S DEAD.

> Green be the graves where her martyrs are lying!
> Shroudless and tombless they sunk to their rest,—
> While o'er their ashes the starry folds flying,
> Wraps the proud eagle they roused from his nest.

—*O. W. Holmes.*

THE SOLDIER'S BURIAL.

Wrap the flag to the soldier's breast;
Into stars and stripes it is stained and blest.
And under the oaks let him rest and rest
    Till God's great Sunday morning.
                    —Battle flag at Shenandoah.

MEMORIAL DAY.

Children bring the buds of Spring time,
Bring the fairest bloom of May.
We will reverently lay them
On the soldiers' graves to-day.
                    —Lizbeth Comings.

AFTER ALL.

The apples are ripe in the orchard,
    The work of the reaper is done,
And the golden woodlands redden
    In the blood of the dying sun.

At the cottage door the grandsire
    Sits, pale, in his easy chair,
While a gentle wind of twilight
    Plays with his silver hair.

A woman is kneeling beside him,
    A fair young head is prest
In the first wild passion of sorrow
    Against his aged breast.

And far from over the distance
    The faltering echos come
Of the flying blast of trumpet
    And the rattling roll of drum.

And the grandsire speaks in a whisper,
    "The end no man can see,
But we give him to his country,
    . And we give our prayers to Thee."

The violets star the meadow,
    The rose-buds fringe the door,
And over the grassy orchard
    The pink-white blossoms pour.

But the grandsire's chair is empty,
    The cottage is dark and still,
There's a nameless grave in the battle-field,
    And a new one under the hill.

And a pallid, tearless woman
    By the cold hearth sits alone,
And the old clock in the corner
    Ticks on with a steady drone.
                     —*William Winter.*

A DAISY'S MISSION.

"I am going to blossom," a daisy said,
"Though the weather is cold and bleak;"
"What for?" said a neighbor, lifting her head,
"It's too early yet by a week."

Said the daisy, "A voice is whispering, 'Speed!'
So I'm wanted somewhere, I know."
"Well, I'm too wise such voices to heed,—
How silly you are to go!"

Memorial day dawned cool and bright,
The sun his warm rays gave,
And there gleamed a star of purest white
On a soldier's lonely grave!
                     —*Youth's Companion.*

SOLDIER'S BURIAL.

Fold him in his country's stars,
Roll the drum and fire the volley!
What to him are all our wars,
What but death-be-mocking folly?

Lay him low, lay him low,
In the clover or the snow,
What cares he? he cannot know.
Lay him low.

—*Geo. H. Boker.*

MY COUNTRY.

With her women of the fairest that bloom beneath the sky,
With her soldiers of the boldest that ever dared to die,
With her flag in glory spreading o'er the earth and o'er the
　　sea—
Like a portent to a tyrant, like a rainbow to the free—
With the nations flowing toward her as to a promised rest—
This, this, of all the lands I saw, is the land I love the best.

—*Everhart.*

SCATTER FLOWERS.

O, children sweet, stay your merry feet,
To gather the blossoms of spring,
And over the graves of our country's braves
Scatter the flowers you bring!

Of the blue or gray, what matter to-day!
For each some fond heart weeps;
So, children dear, make the spot less drear
Wherever a soldier sleeps.

—*Youth's Companion.*

PEACE TO THE BRAVE.

Peace to the brave who nobly fell
'Neath our flag, their hope and pride!
They fought like heroes, long and well,
And then like heroes died.
Nobly they died in freedom's name,
Died our country's flag to save;
Forever sacred be their fame
And green their honored grave.

Harper's.　　　　　　　　　　　　　　　　—*W. T. Adams.*

A SOLDIER'S THOUGHTS.

To-day our thoughts are straying
    As we bow beside our dead,
And we seem to hear the bugle,
    And our massive army tread.

We stand again by the ramparts,
    Where death is raging high,
While the din and smoke of battle
    Rolls up to the blind black sky.

OUR DEAD.

Of man for man the sacrifice,
All that was theirs to give, they gave.
The flowers that blossomed from their graves
Have sown themselves beneath all skies.
                            —*Whittier.*

GARFIELD'S WORDS.

Under the crossed swords and locked shields of Americans,
North and South, our people shall sleep in peace and rise in
liberty and love and harmony under our flag of stars.
                            —*Jas. A. Garfield.*

OUR DEAD HEROES.

These heroes are dead. They died for liberty. They died
for us. They are at rest. They sleep in the land they made
free, under the flag they made stainless, under the solemn
pines, the sad hemlocks, the tearful willows, the embracing
vines.   —*Robt. G. Ingersoll.*

ONE SENTIMENT.

One sentiment for the soldiers living and dead—cheers for
the living and tears for the dead.   —*Robt. G. Ingersoll.*

WHY WE BRING FLOWERS.

They speak of hope to the fainting heart,
With a voice of promise they come and go,
They sleep in the dust through the wintry hours,
They break forth in glory—bring flowers,
Bright flowers.

—Mrs. Hemans.

THE SOLDIER'S SLEEP.

First Child—
How sleep the brave who sink to rest,
By all their country's wishes blest !

—Collins.

Second Child—
He sleeps the iron sleep,
Slain fighting for his country.

—Bryant.

Third Child—
God's finger touched him and he slept.

—Tennyson.

OUR TRIBUTE.

It is little we can do
To show our love for you,
O, warrior blest !
But our choicest, fairest flowers
Shall fall in fragrant showers
Where you rest.

—Youth's Companion.

DECORATION DAY.

Let little hands bring blossoms sweet
To brave men, lying low;
Let little hearts to soldiers dead,
Their love and honor show.

We'll love the flag they loved so well,
The dear old banner bright,
We'll love the land for which they fell
With soul, and strength, and might.

OUR SOLDIERS DEAD.

Gashed with honorable scars,
 Low in glory's lap they lie;
Though they fell, they fell like stars
 Streaming splendor through the sky.
—Montgomery.

THE NAMELESS SLAIN.

First Child—
 On generations yet to be
 Shall break the anthem of the free,

 Forever wafting with its tone
 The names ye carve in crumbling stone;

 Forever bearing—blest refrain !
 The honors of the *nameless slain.*

Second Child—
 Then sleep, ye silent heroes, sleep,
 Through glade and glen, from deep to deep;

 Nor foeman's shaft nor coward's blame
 Shall reach your everlasting fame.
—Henry M. Look.

TO THE LIVING.

Hail to the blue and the gray,
 Who still remain:
United are they to-day,
 Firm friends again.

They fought as brave men fight,
 With conscience clear;
Each thought him in the right
 Nor dreamed of fear.

Fill to the blue and the gray,
 Here's health to all;
Fast friends henceforth are they,
 Whate'er befall.
—Gen. Horatio King.

3

A THOUGHT.

Flowers and songs for the brave who lie
   Under the sculptured stone,
Flowers and tears for the brave unknown;
The missing when battle's storms swept by,
   Somewhere under a watchful sky,
Tho' never a mourner comes to weep,
The Angel of Freedom guards their sleep.

Youth's Companion.   —*Frances L. Mace.*

WASHINGTON IS OUR MODEL.

" Washington is our model,"
   Is the motto we've made for you ;
In the battle of life like him we'll be—
   Brave and generous, kind and true.

" Washington is our model,"
   Is a good model for us all,
Like him we will love this country of ours,
   And be ready to answer her call.

" Washington is our model,"
   Straight and strong and brave,
With eye of light and frame of might,
   And arm of power to save.

" Washington is our model,"
   Upright, firm, and grand,
With kindly face and heart of grace,
   And firm and fearless hand.

—*Journal Education.*

GENERAL WASHINGTON.

Hurrah for General Washington,
   Great man and high,
Who kept his little hatchet bright,
   And never told a lie.

He won us many a battle, boys,
    And set our country free,
And wouldn't we be glad to have
    Another such as he.
             —*Geo. P. Morris.*

THE GOOD OLD DAYS.

When Washington was president,
    As cold as any icicle,
He never on a railroad went,
    And never rode a bicycle.

He read by no electric lamp,
    Nor heard about the Yellowstone,
He never licked a postage stamp,
    And never saw a telephone.

His trousers ended at the knees,
    By wire he could not send dispatch;
He filled his lamp with whale oil grease,
    And never had a match to scratch.

But in these days it's come to pass,
    All work is with such dashing done—
We've all those things ; but then, alas—
    We seem to have no Washington.
             —*Robert J. Burdette.*

WASHINGTON'S MONUMENT.

The wide-spread Republic is the true monument to Washington. Maintain its independence. Uphold its constitution. Preserve its Union. Defend its liberty.
             —*Rob't Chas. Winthrop.*

HONORING WASHINGTON.

Just honor to Washington can only be rendered by observing his precepts and imitating his example.
             —*Rob't Chas. Winthrop.*

WHAT WE KNOW ABOUT WASHINGTON.

All. The birthday of Washington! May it ever be freshly remembered by American hearts.—*Choate.*

First Boy. George Washington was an honest boy who never told a lie.

Second Boy. George Washington was a brave man who fought for his country, liberty and right.

School. Washington whose sword was never drawn but in the cause of his country and never sheathed when wielded in his country's cause.—*J. Q. Adams.*

Third Boy. George Washington was the first president of the United States.

Fourth Boy. He was first in war, first in peace, and first in the hearts of his countrymen.—*Henry Lee.*

Fifth Boy. When Washington died the whole nation mourned because of the loss of so noble and good a man.

———

Have some pupil read the "hatchet story." See STUDENT'S FIRST READER, pp. 85.

———

WASHINGTON'S HISTORY.

[*Have some child read this, as it is too long for the little ones to commit to memory.*]

George Washington, our first president, was inaugurated in New York city on April 30th, 1789, over one hundred years ago.

He lived in Virginia and traveled all the way to New York in a carriage, as there were no railroads in those days. It required eight days to make the journey.

Before he started he went to see his dear old mother to bid her good-bye. He wished the blessing of the one that had taught him so well how to be a great, a noble and an honorable man.

People loved him so well that, everywhere on the road, they greeted him with cheers, flags and flowers.

A splendid vessel, beautifully decorated, carried him across the bay to the city. The bay was filled with gaily trimmed boats and barges. The oars kept time to the music and cannons roared a salute.

Every house in the city, on Washington's route, was garlanded with flowers and evergreens, and draped with flags and silken banners. Everyone waved a hat or a handkerchief, and flowers fell down through the air like snowflakes in a storm.

The name of Washington was everywhere. Bells rang a joyful greeting.

For eight years he was our president, and showed, by his goodness and wisdom, that the people had done well in choosing him for president.

He died at Mt. Vernon in 1799, mourned by the whole country. His last words were: "It is well."

A PRAYER.

God of our sires and sons,
Let other Washingtons
Our country bless,
And, like the brave and wise
Of by-gone centuries,
Show that true greatness lies
In righteousness.

—Pierpont.

WORDS OF WASHINGTON.

When offered soldiers as a body guard our Washington said: "I require no guard but the affections of the people."

WASHINGTON'S STATUE.

O, it was well, in marble firm and white
To carve our hero's form,
Whose angel guidance was our strength in fight,
Our star amid the storm!

—Tuckerman.

WHAT WASHINGTON CONQUERED FOR.

Washington conquered not for fame, but for freedom; not for ambition, but for his country.—*Otis' Eulogy.*

THE BIRTHDAY OF WASHINGTON EVER HONORED.

Welcome, thou festal morn!
Never be passed in scorn
   Thy rising sun,
Thou day forever bright
With Freedom's holy light,
That gave the world the sight
   Of Washington.

Unshaken 'mid the storm,
Behold that noble form—
   That peerless one—
With his protecting hand,
Like Freedom's angel stand,
The guardian of our land,
   Our Washington.

Traced there in lines of light,
Where all pure rays unite,
   Obscured by none;
Brightest on history's page,
Of any clime or age,
As chieftain, man and sage,
   Stands Washington.

Name at which tyrants pale,
And their proud legions quail,
   Their boasting done.
While Freedom lifts her head,
No longer filled with dread,
Her sons to victory led
   By Washington.

Now the true patriot see,
The foremost of the free,
   The victory won,
In Freedom's presence bow,
While sweetly smiling now
She wreathes the spotless brow
   Of Washington.

Then, with each coming year,
Whenever shall appear
    That natal sun,
Will we attest the worth
Of one true man to earth,
And celebrate the birth
    Of Washington.

                                        —*Geo. Howland.*

PAPA'S STORY.

'Twas the night after Christmas, when stuffed full of cake,
And candy and peanuts, each child lay awake.
The stockings were scattered about everywhere,
One could see at a glance that old Nick had been there.
The children were squirming around in their beds,
With pains in their stomachs, and colds in their heads.
Mamma with a bottle, and I with a spoon,
Were watching, and hoping they'd feel better soon.
When in Billy's room there arose such a clatter,
We started—wondered what could be the matter.
Away to the room we sped o'er the floor,
And made no delay to open the door.
The gas was turned low and gave a faint light,
Yet it showed us that Billy was in a great fright.
"O, mamma, be quick, come to me," he cried,
"I've swallowed old Nick and he's kicking inside."
We gave him a dose of hot ginger and whiskey,
He soon went to sleep and ceased to be frisky.
About one o'clock we lay down to sleep,
We think that old "Santa Claus" let us off cheap.

                                        —*Jas. D. Sturges.*

THE CHRISTMAS STORY.

First Child. Among those who came to Bethlehem were a
man and his wife from Nazareth, and as the tavern was crowded
they went to the barn, and there the Chief of children was
born, and cradled in a manger.

And that was the first Christmas.

Second Child.   There were angels without, who brought their glory with them, and they stood and sang, "Glory to God in the highest, and on earth peace to men of good will!"

And that was the first Christmas Carol.

Third Child.   A few shepherds watching their flocks not far away came just as they were, in their every-day clothes, and wondered and glorified, and were glad.

And that was the first Christmas Party.

Fourth Child.   Some travelers from the East were seeking the Christ-child but no one could tell them where he was till a star journeyed on before them, and halted over where the young child was, and they unfolded their treasures, and gave him gold and frankincense and myrrh.

And that was the first Christmas Gift.

Fifth Child.   The shepherds are dead, the "wise men" are in the East, and the angels are in Heaven.   But the star and the child and the manger are everywhere, and they bring a Merry Christmas.

Sixth Child.   Bid the singers begin!   And the same old manger chorus swells sweetly again!   "On earth peace to the men of good will."   Shine on, gentle Star!   All hail, Merry Christmas!—*Vail's Intelligence.*

WHO IS IT ?

Now, children, there's somebody coming
So try and think sharply and well;
And, when I get thro' with my story,
Just see if his name you can tell.

His hair is as white as a snow drift;
But then he is not very old.
His coat is of fur at this season,
The weather, you know, is so cold.

He'll bring all the children a present—
The rich, and, of course, too, the poor.
Some say that he comes down the chimney.
I think he comes in at the door.

COMPLIMENTS OF THE SEASON.

Little Four Years, little Two Years,.
Merry Christmas, Happy New Year's!
That is what I wish for you ;
Shall I tell you what to do
That will make my wish come true ?

Cheerful looks and words are very   ·
Sure to make the Christmas merry ;
Tongues that speak the truth sincere,
Hearts that hold each other dear,
These will make a happy year.

Rossiter W. Raymond.

School Sing—" THE BOOK OF THE NEW YEAR."—*Auntie Em's Songs for Children.*

TOMMY'S DILEMMA.

I want so much on Christmas,
And want it without fail;
I want a rocker-pony
With a "really" mane and tail.

I want a sword and pistol,
And a cap and coat of red;
I want a little wagon
And a double runner sled.

I want a pair of mittens,
For this one's lost its thumb;
I want a book of pictures,
A trumpet and a drum.

And with the nuts and pop-corn,
Sugar plums and all,
I'm just afraid our chimney
Is 'bout a size too small!

SANTA CLAUS AND HIS WORK.

This nice little story for girls and boys
Is all about Santa Claus, Christmas and toys;
So gather around me, but speak not a word—
For I mean what I say by you all shall be heard.
In a nice little city called Santa Clausville,
With its houses and church at the foot of the hill,
Lives jolly old Santa Claus.   Day after day
He works and he whistles the moments away.
You must know he is honest and toils for his bread,
And is fat and good-natured, with nothing to dread.
His eyes are not red, but they twinkle and shine,
For he never was known to drink brandy or wine.
But day after day at his bench he is found,
For he works for all good children all the year round.
Tho' busy all day he is happy and sings
While planning and making the funniest of things,
Such as wagons and horses and dishes and ladles,
And soldiers and monkeys and little dolls' cradles.

—*G. P. Webster.*

LEFT OUT.

One day Saint Nicholas made a complaint:
"I think it is quite plain why they call me a saint.
I wonder if any one happens to see
That nobody ever makes presents to me.
That I, who make presents to ever so many,
Am the only poor fellow who never gets any!"

SANTA CLAUS AND THE MOUSE.

(Concert Recitation for School.)

One Christmas Eve, when Santa Claus
    Came to a certain house,
To fill the children's stockings there,
    He found a little mouse.

"A merry Christmas, little friend,"
  Said Santa, good and kind.
"The same to you, sir," said the mouse.
  "I thought you wouldn't mind

If I should stay awake to-night
  And watch you for a while."
"You're very welcome, little mouse,"
  Said Santa, with a smile.

And then he filled the stockings up
  Before the mouse could wink—
From toe to top, from top to toe,
  There wasn't left a chink.

"Now, they won't hold another thing,"
  Said Santa Claus, with pride.
A twinkle came in mouse's eyes,
  But humbly he replied:

"It's not polite to contradict,
  Your pardon I implore,
But in the fullest stocking there
  I could put one thing more."

"Oh, ho!" laughed Santa. "Silly mouse!
  Don't I know how to pack?
By filling stockings all these years
  I should have learned the knack."

And then he took the stocking down
  From where it hung so high,
And said: "Now put in one thing more;
  I give you leave to try."

The mousie chuckled to himself,
  And then he softly stole
Right to the stocking's crowded toe
  And gnawed a little hole.

"Now, if you please, good Santa Claus,
  I've put in one thing more,

For you will own that little hole
  Was not in there before."

How Santa Claus did laugh and laugh!
  And then he gaily spoke:
" Well! you shall have a Christmas cheese
  For that nice little joke!"

St. Nicholas.   *Emilie Poulsson.*

CHRISTMAS SONG.

Christmas bells!   Christmas bells!
How their merry music swells.
Loud they ring!   Loud they ring!
Santa Claus a welcome bring.
See his sleigh, how packed with toys.
Bells, ring clear!   Bells, ring clear!
Santa Claus is here.

LOOKING FOR SANTA CLAUS.

Small child, with stocking—

Papa, Santa Claus is coming—he is coming soon, I know,
For my mamma says, he always comes to see us with the snow.
And she says, when he is coming, all the bells begin to ring.
Papa, tell me, do you think that he will bring me anything?

See, I've got my stocking, papa—but I think it is so small,
For it won't hold much, my papa—no, it won't hold much at all.
I will go and get my mamma's—I will just go now and see.
Won't you hang it up, my papa—won't you hang it up for me?

I should like to see him, papa, for I heard my mamma tell
How he loved us little children—how he loved us, oh! so well.
Did you ever see him, papa? Mamma says, he's such a sight.
Oh! I wish he'd come soon, papa. Oh! I wish he'd come to-night.

—Jos. D. Turney.

CHRISTMAS EVE.

A STREET SCENE.

[A stocking is seen hanging on the back of a chair. Children wear overcoats, furs and mittens.]

Boy, comes strolling along—Well, if little Tim hasn't hung his stocking up. Such a poor chap as he can't expect to get anything. Santa Claus is only for rich people, as I told him yesterday; and he'll find out that what I tell him is true. [*Goes on.*]

Happy, good-natured boy, comes whistling by; stops abruptly by the stocking—Hello! Here's Tim's stocking [*examines*] and not even so much as a hole in it. I'm sure Santa won't come on *this* back street. It's too bad! [*Puts hands in pockets and thinks.*] I believe I'll put this apple in [*Takes one from his pocket.*], and that will be something. It's a *good* one. Here goes! [*Puts the apple in and walks on. Three girls come along.*]

Jane, pointing—Girls, do look at the stocking that hangs there!

May and Ida, turning—Out of doors, too! Who ever heard of such a thing!

Ida, going nearer—Here's a note!

All—Let's read it.

May, unpins note, opens and reads—DEAR SANTA: I'm Tim. You don't know me, I suppose. I wish you did. Won't you please put something in this stocking for me, just as you do for the other boys? I'll be awful good. I'd like some mittens, and a knife, and a ball, and something for mother. If you haven't these, give me anything, 'cause all the boys say: "Poor boys don't get presents." I can't write, so I had Pete write for me; but he says, I must make my mark, so you'll know it is I. Here it is: +

Jane—Well, this *is* a joke! [*pointing*] See that big cross!

Ida, taking off her mittens—I'm going to put in my mittens!

May—What will your mother say?

Ida—She'll say, "All right."

Jane—If you put mittens in, I must give too, but I haven't a *thing* for a boy.

Ida—Haven't you any money?

Jane—Y-e-s. A dollar that I was going to buy skates with.

May, who has been feeling in her pocket and looking in her purse—I haven't but ten cents. I believe I'll wrap a paper around it, and write "ball" on the outside. [*Does it.*]

All—Just the thing. [*All walk on.*]

Jane, returning—I'll do without the skates. [*Writes on a paper, pins it to the dollar, and says, as she puts it in:*] That's "for mother"—but I did want the skates. [*Runs off.*]

Tim, a little ragged boy, comes slowly to the stocking, glancing cautiously around, takes it quickly, shouting—Hurrah! hurrah! Santa *did* come!

School sing—"BLESSED OLD SANTA CLAUS."—*Auntie Em's Song Leaves.*
—*Helen W. Boyden.*

CHRISTMAS MORNING.

The bells ring clear as bugle note
Sweet song is thrilling every throat,
   'Tis welcome Christmas morning.
Oh, never yet was morn so fair,
Such silent music in the air;
   'Tis merrie Christmas morning.

Dear day of all days in the year.
Dear day of song, good will, and cheer.
   'Tis golden Christmas morning.
The Hope, the Faith, the Love that is,
The Peace, the holy Promises,
   'Tis glorious Christmas morning.
—*Joaquin Miller.*

A CHRISTMAS TREE FAIRY.

I know a little fairy,
A kind good fairy she,
Who comes to us at Christmas time,
And brings the Christmas tree.
She is the sweetest fairy
In all the fairy books,
Altho' I've never seen her,
And I don't know how she looks.

I dreamt last night the fairy came and brought the Christmas
    tree,
And in her arms she carried a little doll for me,
A dolly with a blue silk dress and lovely golden hair,
You never saw a sweeter little dolly anywhere.
And mother says, if I am very good at work and play,
She thinks the fairy means to bring a doll on Christmas day.
    Song Daisy.   *—Lizzie and R. E. Mack.*

WELCOME NEW YEAR.

Now welcome, welcome, glad New Year!
    Dawn brightly on us all,
And bring us hope our hearts to cheer,
    Whatever may befall.
Bring patience, comfort, gladness, rest;
    Bring blessings from above;
Bring happiness, the brightest, best—
    To us and those we love.

A HAPPY NEW YEAR.

A right good year,
    And a merry good year!
And a joy for each day the year has in it,
    And a smile to beguile
    All sorrow the while,
And the love of all, with the gift to win it.
                    —E. Sigourney.

WHAT THE BELLS SAID.

Then pealed the bells more loud and deep:
"God is not dead, nor doth he sleep!
    The wrong shall fail,
    The right prevail,
With peace on earth, good will to men."
                    —Longfellow.

A WINTER SONG.

Girl—Oh, Summer has the roses
            And the laughing light south wind,
            And the merry meadows lined
With dewy, dancing posies.

Boy—   But Winter has the sprites
            And the witching frosty nights.

Girl—Oh, Summer has the splendor
            Of the cornfields wide and deep,
            Where scarlet poppies sleep
And wavy shadows wander.

Boy—   But Winter fields are rare
            With diamonds everywhere.

Girl—Oh, Summer has the wild bees,
            And the ringing, ringing note
            In the robin's tuneful throat,
And the leaf-talk in the trees.

Boy—   But Winter has the chime
            Of the merry Christmas time.

Girl—Oh, Summer has the lustre
            Of the sunbeams warm and bright,
            And rains that fall at night
Where reeds and lilies cluster.

Boy—   But deep in Winter's snow
            The fires of Christmas glow.

St. Nicholas   *Susan Hartley.*

DO THE BEST YOU CAN.

And this, if you have but little,
Is what I would say to you:
Make all you can of that little—
Do all the good you can do.

And though your gifts be humble,
Let no little child, I pray,
Find only an empty stocking
On the morn of Christmas day!

—Phoebe Cary.

CHRISTMAS.

Heap on more wood! The wind is chill;
But, let it whistle as it will,
We'll keep our Christmas merry still.
Each age has deemed the new-born year
The fittest time for festal cheer.
And well our Christian sires of old
Loved when the year its course had rolled,
And brought blithe Christmas back again,
With all its hospitable train.

—Sir Walter Scott.

CHRISTMAS DAY.

All the bells on earth shall ring,
On Christmas day, on Christmas day,
And all the bells on earth shall ring,
On Christmas day in the morning.

CHRISTMAS IS COME.

The old north breeze thro' the skeleton trees
Is chanting the year out drearily;
But loud let it blow, for at home, we know,
That the dry logs crackle cheerily,
And the frozen ground is in fetters bound.
But pile up the wood—we can burn it;
For Christmas is come and in every home
To summer our hearts can turn it.

—Albert Smith.

CHRISTMAS.

A merry, merry Christmas!
To crown the closing year;
Peace and good-will to mortals,
And words of holy cheer.

What tho' the dreary landscape
Be robed in drifting snow,
If on the social hearthstone
The Christmas fires may glow?

What tho' the wind at evening
Blow harsh o'er land and sea,
If eager hands and joyful
Light up the Christmas tree?

"'TWAS THE NIGHT BEFORE CHRISTMAS."

One night I thought to take a peep
   While Santa Claus was near me,
For when he thought I was asleep
   I knew he would not hear me.

No doubt you think his merry looks
   You'd recognize instanter;
You've seen him in the picture-book
   With reindeer on a canter!

That I should know him anywhere
   I felt profoundly certain,
So, cautiously, while he was there,
   I folded back the curtain.

And then I looked for Santa Claus,
   Nor dreamed I'd see another.
Now, who do you suppose it was?
   Why, bless you, 'twas MY MOTHER!

ON CHRISTMAS.

First Child—

Those Christmas bells so sweetly chime
As on the day when first they rung
So merrily in the olden time,
And far and wide their music flung.
They still proclaim to every ear,
Old Christmas comes but once a year.

Second Child—

The poor will many a care forget,
The debtor think not of his debt ;
But, as they each enjoy their cheer,
Wish it was Christmas all the year.

Third Child—

The children of the poor
For once are happy all day long.
We smile and listen to the song,
The burden still remote or near,
" Old Christmas comes but once a year."

All—

Then let us sing amid our cheer,
Old Christmas comes but once a year.

—Selected from Thos. Miller.

A CHRISTMAS WISH.

Now Christmas comes with hearty cheer,
May kindly thoughts go round,
And bring to you a glad New Year,
With peace and plenty crowned.

A THANKSGIVING TALE.

[Grandma, with folded kerchief, cap and spectacles, sits knitting when the children come in.]

Grandma—Come, children, sit around me while I tell you a Thanksgiving story. [*Children draw chairs around her, saying:*]

Boy—		O, ho! that's what *I* like.
Fan—	*together*	'Course we will.
Lucy—		How good you are.

Grandma—A long, long time ago, before my grandma was born, a ship came sailing over the sea to Plymouth rock.

Boy—Whew! that *was* a long time ago.

Fan—Keep still! Grandma can't tell us the story if you keep talking all the time.

Lucy—Go on, grandma. Were they "the Pilgrims"?

Grandma—Yes, child. They built log houses with high log fences around them to keep the savage Indians away.

Fan—I've seen the pictures of those queer fences. The logs were pointed at the top.

Boy—Who's talking *now?*

Lucy—You!

Grandma—The Pilgrims worked very hard, planting corn and grain for food in the coming winter. But many sickened and died. The crops were poor and scanty,—

Lucy, interrupting—When they buried the dead they sowed grain over the graves, so the Indians could not find them. Didn't they, grandma?

Grandma—Yes, dear. But a time came when there was little to eat, and they knew not where to get more. So they all prayed to God to send help before they starved. Soon they saw a ship.

Fan—How glad they must have been!

Grandma—The vessel brought plenty and to spare. The people set aside a day to give thanks to God for his many kindnesses.

Lucy—Giving thanks—that's what Thanksgiving means, isn't it?

Boy, jumping up and sniffing—I smell turkey; wonder if it is done! [*Children go out, and Grandma follows slowly.*]

—Helen W. Boyden.

A HYMN.

First Girl, with wreath of asters—

> Thanksgiving for the care
> That plants the aster fair
> By dusty waysides where tired feet must stray.
> Star thoughts that light the way.

Second Girl, wreath of woodbine—
>For flaming banners hung
>Our swamps and woods among;
>For bowers of clematis, for woodbine's grace,
>Sing praise, sing praise.

Third Girl, wreath of autumn leaves—
>For lanes made color-glad,
>For trees with radiance clad,
>For peerless cardinal flowers, whose glowing ranks
>Guard the still brook, give thanks.

All—
>Sing, heart, be glad and sing;
>For know, O, heart, the King
>Desires thy beauty. Join thou in His praise
>Thro' all the autumn days.

Journal Education. ——— *—Sarah L. Arnold.*

FRED'S SPEECH.

To-morrow will be "Thanksgiving day." The Yankees are a very ingenious people; they get a great many patents. They invented "Thanksgiving day," but did not get any patent for it. I suppose there was no patent office then, or they would have done so. "Thanksgiving day" is one of the best things they have ever invented. All of the States have to have it now. It comes just at the right time of the year. Just when turkeys and mince pies are ripe, and when cider has what the Yankees call, "Just a leetle *tang.*"

Everybody ought to be thankful *all the time* for what they have and for what they have not.

I'm thankful that I have a good father and mother, and that my mother-in-law thinks I'm all right. I'm thankful that I've a good appetite and plenty to eat, and that I have *not* the measles.

Everybody ought to be thankful for "Thanksgiving day." The farmer, because it raises the price of turkeys; we boys, and all the other bankers, because it gives us a holiday.

I hope all the teachers and children in this school will have a good time to-morrow. The doctors' Thanksgiving will come the day after. *—Jas. D. Sturges.*

LITTLE PAUL'S THANKSGIVING.

They tossed him and they squeezed him;
　They kissed him, one and all.
They said, " You blessed, blessed boy!"
　And, " Darling little Paul!"

But they didn't give him any turkey
　Nor any pumpkin pie,
And when the nuts and grapes came round
　They slyly passed him by.

But he didn't seem to mind it,
　For, in the sweetest way,
He sat and sucked his thumb
　His *first Thanksgiving day!*

THANKSGIVING TURKEY.

(Concert Recitation for School.)

I knew a little turkey who
　Was never satisfied.
He ate and ate, and grew and grew,
　And wanted more beside.

His parents reprimanded him,
　And said he'd come to grief.
Said he: "Old folks are very prim,
　And that is *my* belief. "

He robbed the chickens of their share;
　Assaulted Mrs. Hen;
And killed her only son and heir,
　No bigger than a wren.

He challenged Mr. Chanticleer,
　When he was but a youth;
Then greedily beside his bier
　He ate, and that's the truth.

He fought with ducklings and with geese
  And kept them all in fear,
Till there was never any peace
  When he was standing near.

He ate the farmer's corn and wheat,
  He ate the peas and beans;
He was a greedy, greedy cheat
  And lived beyond his means.

He grew so very corpulent
  The farmer wagged his head;
The barnyard gossips said it meant
  That fowl was good as dead.

And when to gobbler's high estate
  He did arrive, at last,
They warned him ere it was too late
  To pause and think and fast.

He gobbled all their words to scorn
  And went his greedy way,
Until, one cold and frosty morn
  Before Thanksgiving Day,

The farmer, oh! he did appear,
  And with an ax he slew
That gobbler; but no single tear
  His death-bed did bedew.

The fowls within the farm-yard beat
  Their wings, and quacked and crew,
The farmer's relatives did eat
  That turkey.   So did you.

                          —*Lizzie Burt.*

WE PRAISE THEE.

For the sun-ripened fruit and the billowy grain,
For the orange and apple, the corn and the cane,
For the bountiful harvest now gathered and stored,
That by Thee in the lap of the nation were poured,
            We praise Thee, gracious God.

GIVING.

God loveth the cheerful giver,
   Tho' the gift be poor and small;
What doth he think of his children
   When they never give at all?

A REQUEST.

O, Father, bless the gifts we bring!
   Cause Thou Thy face to shine,
Till every nation owns her King,
   And all the earth is Thine.

            —*O. W. Holmes.*

THANKSGIVING.

Thank God for rest, where none molest,
   And none can make afraid,—
For Peace that sits as Plenty's guest
   Beneath the homestead shade.

            —*Whittier.*

BUILD UP AN ALTAR.

Build up an altar to the Lord,
   O, grateful heart of ours!
And shape it of the greenest sward
   That ever drank the showers.

Lay all the bloom of gardens there,
   And there the orchard fruits;
Bring golden grain from sun and air,
   From earth her goodly roots.

            —*Whittier.*

OUR COUNTRY.

Great God! we thank Thee for this home,
   This bounteous birth-land of the free;
Where wanderers from afar may come,
   And breathe the air of liberty!   — *Pabodie.*

THE REASON WHY.

" We learn it all in hist'ry. You didn't think I knew?
Why don't you s'pose I study my lessons? *Course* I do.
The Pilgrim Fathers did it; they made Thanksgiving Day.
Why? Oh, I don't remember; my hist'ry doesn't say.
Or p'r'aps I wasn't listening when she was telling why;
But if the Pilgrim Mothers were busy making pie,
I s'pose they couldn't bother, and so that was the way
It happened that the *Fathers* made our Thanksgiving Day."
—*J. M. L.*

THANKSGIVING.

First Child—
  Let us thank Him for the rose,
   Which the summer season lends;
  For each blade of grass that grows
   And the sunshine that He sends;

Second Child—
  For the daisies' drift of snow,
   And the sunflower's golden shields;
  For the strawberry-plants that sow
   Small white stars throughout the fields;

Third Child—
  For the thistle's purple crown,
   And the hawkweed's yellow hood;
  For the crocus in its gown,
   And the wild bird in the wood.

Fourth Child—
  For the milk-weed, spilling out
   All its hoard of silken skeins;
  For the brooks that sing and laugh
   Louder after heavy rains;

Fifth Child—
  For the stars that nightly rise,
   All the heavens brimming;
  For the rainbow in the skies,
   And the cricket's hymning.

Sixth Child—

> Thank Him for the red leaf's glow,
>   For the vine's increase,
> For the promise of the snow,
>   And the wide world's lease !

> —*Mary A. Prescott.*

NEW VERSION SPIDER AND FLY.

First Pupil—

> "Will you walk into my parlor?"
>   Said the spider to the fly;
> "Tis the prettiest little parlor
>   That ever you did spy."

Second Pupil—

> The spider is the rumseller,
>   And the fly the foolish man
> The rumseller intends to catch,
>   If by any means he can.

First Pupil—

> "The way into my parlor
>   Is up a winding stair;
> And I've many, many pretty things
>   To show you when you're there."

Second Pupil—

> It is a winding stair indeed,
>   But it windeth down, not up;
> And his foot is on the fatal stair
>   Who sips the sparkling cup.

First Pupil—

> Said the cunning spider to the fly:
>   "Dear friend, what shall I do
> To prove the warm affection
>   I have always felt for you?"

Third Pupil—

> Alas! alas! how very soon
>   This silly little fly,
> Hearing his wily, flattering words,
>   Came slowly flitting by.

He dragged her up his winding stair
    Into his dismal den,
Within his little parlor;
    But *she* never came out again.

Second Pupil—

    Behold the end, the bitter end,
       Of those who love the bowl,
    Shut out from all that life holds dear,
       Wrecked body, mind, and soul.

—Lizzie T. Larkin.

THE REASON WHY.

There was an old woman, and what do you think,
She has bread to eat and milk to drink,
Clothes and home and best of diet,
Yet she was sad, and couldn't be quiet.
She was sad in her heart over very bad laws,
And she worked night and day in the Temperance cause.
"If they wouldn't make whiskey and sell it," said she,
"Not a beggar or drunkard abroad would I see."

—Mrs. J. McNair Wright.

School Sing—

"PITCHER OR JUG?"

—Auntie Em's Songs for Children.

FROM A MAN TO A JUG.

First Girl—

    Give ear, we beg you, to our song
    We will try not to make it very long,
    'Bout a man who loved strong drink,
    So, so very silly a man we think.

All Four Sing. Tune. LITTLE BROWN JUG.

    O, no, no drink for me [1]
    Unless it's water pure and free.
    O, no, no drink for me [1]
    Unless it's water pure and free,

[1] Move heads from side.

Second Girl—

This man—a brute, at home, abroad,
He loved not man and he loved not his God.
He'd make children to him bring
His jug of cider, then he would sing:

Sing—

Ha! ha! ha! you and me [2]
Little brown jug, don't I love thee?

Third Girl—

He drank and drank, so people said,
Till his hair grew white [3] and his nose [4] grew red;
He was coarse, his voice was gruff,
Still he drank, but he couldn't drink enough.

Four Girls Sing—

O, no, no, etc.

Fourth Girl—

A sad, sad fate they say befell
Just like a big, big jug he soon did swell,
His arms were stiff like handles, too, [5]
His head to a wooden stopper grew. [6]

Four Girls Sing—

O, no, no, etc.

—Annie Chase.

[2] Throw back heads and smile. [3] Touch hair with right hand. [4] Touch nose with right hand. [5] Arms akimbo. [6] Touch head, making slight bow.

TEMPERANCE SONG.

First Child—

When the bright morning star the new daylight is bringing,
And the orchards and groves are with melody ringing,
Their way to and from them the early birds winging,
And their anthems of gladness and thanksgiving singing;
Why do they so twitter and sing, do you think?
Because they've had nothing but water to drink.

Second Child—

When a shower on a hot day in summer is over,
And the fields are all smelling of white and red clover,

And the honey-bee—busy and plundering rover—
Is fumbling the blossom leaves over and over,
    Why so fresh, clean and sweet are the fields, do you think?
    Because they've had nothing but water to drink.

Third Child—
Do you see that stout oak on its windy hill growing?
Do you see what great hailstones that black cloud is throwing?
Do you see that steam war-ship its ocean way going,
Against trade-winds and head-winds like hurricanes blowing?
    Why are oaks, cloud and war-ships so strong, do you
        think?
    Because they've had nothing but water to drink.

Fourth Child—
Now if *we* have to work in the shop, field, or study,
And would have a strong hand and a cheek that is ruddy,
And would *not* have a brain that is addled and muddy,
With our eyes all bunged up, and our noses all bloody—
    How shall *we* make and keep ourselves so, do you think?
    Why, *we* must have nothing but water to drink.
                              —*John Pierpont.*

School Sing—
          " WHAT SAYETH THEY?"
            —*Auntie Em's Songs For Children.*

TO TAKE IT IS FOLLY.

Strong drink is a sower
    Of malice and strife,
A poison that cankers
    The fountains of life.

Strong drink's a deceiver,
    As thousands have found;
He tells men that pleasure
    With him shall abound.

Strong drink is a jailer;
    Ah! has he not bound
Ten thousand poor drunkards
    Like slaves to the ground?
                        —*Banner of Light.*

"THE PLANTING OF THE APPLE TREE."

First Girl—

> Come, let us plant the apple tree,
> Cleave the tough greensward with the spade;
> Wide let its hollow bed be made;
> There lay the roots, and there
> Sift the dark mold with kindly care,
> And press it o'er them tenderly,
> As round the sleeping infant's feet
> We softly fold the cradle sheet;
> So plant we the apple tree.

Second Girl—

> What plant we in this apple tree?
> Buds, which the breath of summer days,
> Shall lengthen into leafy sprays;
> Boughs where the thrush, with crimson breast,
> Shall haunt and sing and hide her nest;
> We plant upon the sunny lea,
> A shadow for the noontide hour,
> A shelter from the summer shower,
> When we plant the apple tree.

Third Girl—

> What plant we in this apple tree?
> Sweets for a hundred flowery springs,
> To load the May wind's restless wings,
> When, from the orchard row he pours,
> Its fragrance through our open doors;
> A world of blossoms for the bee,
> Flowers for the sick girl's silent room,
> For the glad infant sprigs of bloom,
> We plant with the apple tree.

Fourth Girl—

> What plant we in this apple tree?
> Fruits that shall swell in sunny June,
> And redden in the August noon,
> And drop when gentle airs come by,
> That fan the blue September sky,
> While children come with cries of glee,

And seek them where the fragrant grass,
Betrays their bed to those who pass,
At the foot of the apple tree.

Fifth Girl—

The fruitage of this apple tree,
Winds and our flag of stripe and star
Shall bear to coasts that lie afar,
Where men shall wonder at the view,
And ask in what fair groves they grew;
And sojourners beyond the sea,
Shall think of childhood's careless day
And long, long hours of summer play,
In the shade of the apple tree.

Sixth Girl—

Each year shall give this apple tree,
A broader flush of roseate bloom,
A deeper maze of verdurous gloom,
And loosen when the frost clouds lower,
The crisp brown leaves in thicker shower,
The years shall come and pass, but we
Shall hear no longer, where we lie,
The summer's song, the autumn's sigh,
In the boughs of the apple tree.

Seventh Girl—

" Who planted this old apple tree ? "
The children of that distant day
Thus to some aged man shall say;
And gazing on its mossy stem,
The gray-haired man shall answer them:
" A poet of the land was he,
Born in the rude but good old times;
' Tis said he made some quaint old rhymes
On planting the apple tree."

—*William Cullen Bryant.*

PLANT TREES.

Plant trees, plant trees on Arbor Day,
  Along the shadeless, dusty way;

Who plants a tree shall surely be
A blessing to humanity.

—Youth's Companion.

THE ELM.

Hail to the elm! the brave old elm!
    Our last lone Forest tree,
Whose limbs outstand the lightning's brand,
    For a brave old elm is he!
For fifteen score of full-told years
    He has borne his leafy prime,
Yet he holds them well, and lives to tell
    His tale of the olden time!
Then hail to the elm! the green-topped elm!
    And long may his branches wave,
For a relic is he, the gnarled old tree,
    Of the times of the good and brave.

—N. S. Dodge.

PLANTING TREES.

First Boy—

    If we are all to choose and say,
    What trees we'd like to plant to-day,
        Seems to me
        None can be
    Half so good as a Christmas tree!
    For surely even a baby knows
    That's where the nicest candy grows.
        Candy on a Christmas tree—
        That's what pleases me!

Second Boy—

    Planted out 'twould never bear—
    But after all, why should we care?
        The richest thing
        Is what we bring
    From sugar maples in the Spring.
    So now I'll set a Maple here,
    For feast and frolic every year.
        Sugar from a Maple tree
        That's what pleases me!

Third Boy—

> Sweets are good 'most any day,
> But as for trees I'm bound to say,
> A shag bark tall
> Is best of all
> When once the trees begin to fall;
> And so a Hickory tree I'll set
> And piles of fun and nuts I'll get.
> Nuts from a Hickory tree—
> That's what pleases me!

Fourth Boy—

> I shall plant an apple tree,
> That's the best of all for me;
> And each kind
> To suit my mind
> On this one with grafts I'll bind.
> Ripe or green the whole year thro';
> Pie or dumpling, bake or stew,
> Every way I like 'em best,
> And I'll treat the rest.

Youth's Companion.   *—Eudora S. Bunstead.*

WHAT A BIRD SAID.

> " Why do you come to my apple tree,
>   Little bird so grey?"
> Twit-twit, twit-twit, twit-twit, twee!
>   That was all he would say.

> " Why do you lock your rosy feet
>   So closely round the spray?"
> Twit-twit, twit-twit, twit-tweet!
>   That was all he would say.

> " Why on the top-most bough do you get,
>   Little bird so grey?"
> Twit-twit-twee, twit-twit-twit!
>   That was all he would say.

5

" Where is your mate?　Come answer me,
　Little bird so grey."
Twit-twit-twit! twit-twit-twee!
　That was all he would say.

" And has she little rosy feet?
　And is her body grey?"
Twit-twit! twit-twit-tweet!
　That was all he would say.

" And will she come with you and sit
　In my apple tree some day?"
Twit-twit-tweet! twit-twit-twit!
　He said as he flew away.

—Alice Cary.

HARK! HARK!

Large Girl—

　　Hark! hark! my children, hark!
　　When the sky has lost its blue,
　　What do the stars say in the dark?

Children—

　　We must sparkle, sparkle through.

Large Girl—

　　What do the leaves say in the storm,
　　Tossed in whispering heaps together?

Children—

　　We must keep the violets warm,
　　Till they wake in fairer weather.

Large Girl—

　　What do little birdies say,
　　Flitting thro' the gloomy wood?

Children—

　　We must sing the gloom away;
　　Sun or shadow, God is good.

THE TREE.

The tree's early leaf-buds were bursting their brown;
" Shall I take them away?" said the frost, sweeping down
" No, leave them alone,
Till the blossoms have grown,"
Prayed the tree while he trembled
From leaflet to crown.

The tree bore his blossoms and all the birds sung.
" Shall I take them away?" said the wind as he swung.
" No! leave them alone,
Till the berries have grown,"
Said the tree, while his leaflets quivering hung.

The Tree bore his fruit in the midsummer glow;
Said the girl, " May I gather thy berries now?"
" Yes, all thou canst see;
Take them, all are for thee,"
Said the tree, while he bent down his laden boughs low.

—Bjornsteine Bjornson.

TO A HONEY-BEE.

" Busy-body, busy-body,
    Always on the wing,
Wait a bit, where you have lit,
    And tell me why you sing?"

Up and in the air again,
    Flap, flap, flap!
And now she stops and now she drops
    Into the rose's lap.

" Come, just a minute come,
    From your rose so red,"
Hum, hum, hum, hum—
    That was all she said.

" Busy-body, busy-body,
    Always light and gay.
It seems to me, for all I see,
    Your work is only play."

" Come, just a moment come,
   From your rosy bed."
Hum, hum, hum, hum
   That was all she said.

—Alice Cary.

SUNSHINE.

Boy—

Good morning, merry sunshine!
   How did you wake so soon?
You've scared away the little stars
   And hid the pretty moon.

I saw you go to sleep last night,
   Before I ceased my playing.
How did you get away over here,
   And where have you been staying?

Fair Little Girl—

I never go to sleep, dear child,
   I just go around to see
My little children in the East
   Who rise and watch for me.

I waken all the birds and bees,
   And flowers on my way;
And last of all the little boy
   Who stayed out late to play.

ROOM AT THE TOP.

Never you mind the crowd, boys,
   Or fancy your life won't tell;
The work is the work for all that
   To him that doeth it well.
Fancy the world a hill, boys;
   Look where the millions stop!
You'll find the crowd at the base, boys,
   There's always room at the top.

SPIDER AND FLY.

Once when morn was flowing in,
  Broader, redder, wider,
In her house with walls so thin
  That they could not hide her,
Just as she would never spin,
  Sat a little spider—
Sat she on her silver stairs,
  Meek as if she said her prayers.

Came a fly whose wings had been
  Making circles wider,
Having but the buzz and din
  Of herself to guide her.
Nearer to these walls so thin,
  Nearer to the spider,
Sitting on her silver stairs,
  Meek as if she said her prayers.

Said the silly fly: " Too long
  Malice has belied her;
How should she do any wrong,
  With no walls to hide her?"
So she buzzed her pretty song
  To the wily spider,
Sitting on her silver stairs
  Meek as though she said her prayers.

But in spite her modest mien,
  Had the fly but eyed her
Close enough, she would have seen
  Fame had not belied her—
That, as she had always been,
  She was still a spider;
And that she was not at prayers,
  Sitting on her silver stairs.

—Alice Cary.

———

DANDELION'S SAD STORY.

There was a pretty dandelion,
  With lovely, fluffy hair,

That glistened in the sunshine
  And in the summer air.
But, oh! this pretty dandelion
  Soon grew quite old and gray;
And, sad to tell! her charming hair
  Blew many miles away.

               —G. W. Chadwick.

GOOD MORNING.

Good morning! good morning, the birdies sing;
  Good-by to the windy days of spring!
The sun is so bright that we must be gay.
  Good morning! good morning! this glad summer day.

A PEARL.

Wise sayings often fall to the ground, but kind words never die.

A SHORT SERMON.

Be you tempted as you may,
Each day and every day,
  Speak what is true!
True things, in great and small;
Then, though the sky should fall,
Sun, moon and stars and all,
  Heaven would show through!

               —Alice Cary.

THE MOUNTAIN AND THE SQUIRREL.

The Mountain and the Squirrel
  Had a quarrel;
For the former called the latter " Little Prig."
  Bun replied:
" You are doubtless very big,
But all sorts of things and weather

Must be taken in together
To make up a year and a sphere;
And I think it no disgrace
To occupy my place.
If I'm not as large as you,
You are not as small as I,
Nor half so spry;
I'll not deny you make
A very pretty squirrel track.
Talents differ, all is well and wisely put.
If I cannot carry forests on my back,
Neither can you crack a nut."

—Emerson.

THE SEASONS.

A Tiny Girl—

The flowery Spring leads sunny Summer,
And yellow Autumn presses near,
Then in his turn comes gloomy Winter
Till smiling Spring again appear.

—Burns.

First Child—

Spring the sweet spring, is the year's pleasant King;
Then blooms each thing, then maids dance in a ring,
Cold doth not sting, the pretty birds do sing.

—Thos. Nash.

Second Child—

Child of the Sun, refulgent Summer comes,
In pride of youth and felt thro' Nature's depths:
He comes attended by the sultry hours;
And ever fanning breezes on his way.

—Thomson

Third Child—

Autumn's sighing,
Moaning, dying;
Clouds are flying
On like steeds;
While their shadows

O'er the meadows
Walk like widows
Decked in weeds.   *—T. Buchanan Read.*

Fourth Child—

A wrinkled, crabbed man they picture thee,
Old Winter, with thy rugged beard as gray
As the long moss upon the apple tree;
Blue lipt, an ice-drop at thy sharp blue nose
Close muffled up, and on thy dreary way,
Plodding alone thro' sleet and drifting snows.

—Southey.

GOOD ADVICE.

Cherish what is good and drive
Evil thoughts and feelings far;
For, as sure as you're alive,
You will show for what you are.

—Alice Cary.

EARLY RISING.

First Child—

He who would thrive
Must rise at five.

Second Child—

He who would thrive still more
Must rise at stroke of four.

Third Child—

He who'd still more thriving be
Must leave his bed at turn of three.

Fourth Child—

And who this latter would outdo,
Will rouse him at the stroke of two.

Fifth Child—

Who would never be outdone,
Must ever rise as soon as one.

Sixth Child—

He who'd flourish best of all,
Must never go to bed at all.

THE FAITHFUL CLOCK.

Altho' my hands are on my face,
And all the time I go on tick,
Trust me, mine is a worthy case;
The slow may think I'm quick,
But fast and slow at once may see
At any time good works in me.

Harpers' Weekly.   —*Geo. W. Bungay.*

ONLY.

Only a drop in the bucket,
  But every drop will tell;
The bucket would soon be empty
  Without the drops in the well.

THE WISEST WAY.

Do your best, your very best,
  And do it every day;
Little boys and little girls,
  That is the wisest way.

CHERRIES.

Under the tree the farmer said,
Smiling and shaking his wise old head:
"Cherries are ripe, but then you know,
There's the grass to cut and the corn to hoe;
We can gather the cherries any day,
But when the sun shines we must make our hay;
To-night, when the work has all been done,
We'll muster the boys for fruit and fun."

Up in a tree a robin said,
Perking and cocking his saucy head;
"Cherries are ripe! and so to-day,
We'll gather them while you make the hay;

For we are the boys with no corn to hoe,
No cows to milk, and no grass to mow."
At night the farmer said: "Here's a trick!
These roguish robins have had their pick."
—*Emily Huntington Miller.*

A STITCH DROPPED.

Grandma sat busily knitting away,
A trim little stocking, all scarlet and gray;
Katy stood leaning on grandma's knee,
Anxiously waiting and watching to see
How quickly the pretty stripes could grow,
With grandma's fingers a-flying so.

All at once, in a round of gray,
The busy needles ceased their play.
"Dear me!" said grandma, "I can't tell which,
But somewhere here I have dropped a stitch;
And I cannot see, it has grown so late,
To pick it up; so we must wait

"Till the lamps come in." Down Katy went,
Moved by a sudden kind intent;
Down in the fire-light on the floor,
Searching the hearth-rug o'er and o'er.
"What are you looking for, my child?"
Mamma questioned and slyly smiled.

Soberly answered the little witch,
"I'm trying to find my grandma's stitch!"
—*Youth's Companion.*

TWO THINGS.

Two things we should never fret about, first, what we *can* prevent; and second what we *cannot* prevent.

BIRDS IN SUMMER.

How pleasant the life of a bird must be,
Flitting about in each leafy tree!
In the leafy trees so broad and tall,

Like a green and beautiful palace hall,
With its airy chambers light and fair,
That open to sun and stars and moon;
That open unto the bright blue sky,
And the frolicsome winds as they wander by!
—*Mary Howitt.*

TO MOTHER FAIRIE.

Good old mother Fairie,
  Sitting by your fire,
Have you any little folk
  You would like to hire?

I want no chubby drudges
  To milk and churn and spin,
Nor old and wrinkled Brownies,
  With grisly beards, and thin;

But patient little people,
  With hands of busy care,
And gentle speech, and loving hearts;
  Say, have you such to spare?
—*Alice Cary.*

TELLING BIDDY THE NEWS.

I've got the best news for you, biddy!
Stop cackling this minute and hear.
Our baby has cutted a tooths, biddy,
The darlingest little dear!

It doesn't show much, but it *feels*, biddy;
I feeled it free minutes ago.
It's little and shiny and sharp, biddy,
And 'sides, you know, it'll *grow.*

Oh, hum! seems 'sif I must jump, biddy,
It's such a beautiful thing!
Let's celebrate—me and you, biddy,
You cackle, biddy, and I'll sing.

    *   *   *   *   *

There now, let me look at *your* tooths, biddy,
Why, there hasn't a single one grew!
Aren't you 'shamed as you can be, biddy,
A great old hen like you!

But may be, it's 'cause you *are* old, biddy,
And I'm sorry as I can be.
We'll go to the toothman's, biddy,
And I'll tell him to put in free.

     *   *   *   *   *

But I 'most forgot 'bout the baby,
Guess I must run and see.
May be another tooths come, biddy,
O, my! who knows but there's *free!*

Youth's Companion.   —*A. H. Donnell.*

WHAT MOTHER SAYS.

Now here's a handglass; let me try
If I can this time see
Just one of those funny things
My Mother sees in me.

She says my eyes are violets—
And what she says is true—
But *I* think they are just two eyes;
Don't they look so to *you?*

She says my lips are cherries red,
And makes b'lieve, take a bite.
They never look like *that* to me—
But Mother's *always* right.

She says, each cheek is like a rose;
And this I *surely* know,
I never would believe it—but
What *Mother* says is so.

She says, my teeth are shining pearls;
Now that's so very queer,
If *some* folks said it, why, I'd think—
But then, 'twas Mother dear.

I only see a little girl,
With hair that's rather wild,
Who has two eyes, a nose and mouth,
Like any other child.

Poetry and Pictures.   —*Lizbeth B. Comings.*

GOING TO SLEEP.

First Child—

How does the lily go to sleep
In its silver cradle smooth and deep?

Second Child—

Clouds of purple, crimson, gold,
Melt in azure, fold on fold;
Stars look down, so mild and clear;
Sweet winds whisper: "By lo, dear!"
So the lily goes to sleep
In its silver cradle, smooth and deep.

First Child—

How does the robin go to sleep
In its leafy cradle, soft and deep?

Third Child—

Fainter shines the daisied hill;
One by one the songs grow still.
On the tree-top, safe and high,
Leaves are lisping: "Rock-a-bye!"
So the robin goes to sleep
In its leafy cradle, soft and deep.

First Child—

How does the baby go to sleep
In its downy cradle, soft and deep?

Fourth Child—

Pearly eyelids gently close,
As the leaflets of the rose;
Mother fondly watches nigh,
Softly singing: "Lullaby!"

So the baby goes to sleep
In its downy cradle, warm and deep.

First Child—

Who is it watches while they sleep
In their nightly cradles, calm and deep?

All—

O, the Father's loving care
For His children everywhere!
Baby, lily, robin, rest
Safely on His boundless breast!
So He watches while they sleep
In their nightly cradles, calm and deep.

—*Poetry and Pictures.*

SUPPOSE.

How dreary would the meadows be
In the pleasant summer light,
Suppose there wasn't a bird to sing,
And suppose the grass was white!

And what would all the beauty be,
And what the song that cheers,
Suppose we hadn't any eyes,
And suppose we hadn't any ears?

Ah, think of it, my little friends;
And when some pleasure flies,
Why, let it go, and still be glad
That you have ears and eyes.

—*Alice Cary.*

THE MONTHS.

[*For Twelve Little Ones.*]

First Child—

January, icy cold,
Leaves a mantle soft and white;

Second Child—

> February, sharp and bold,
> Onward takes his busy flight.

Third Child—

> March's chilly breezes blow,
> Still they're touched by Winter's hand;

Fourth Child—

> April melts the frozen snow;
> April sunshine floods the land.

Fifth Child—

> May awakes the sleeping flowers,
> Reigns a sweet and happy queen;
> With her coaxing sun and showers
> Robes the trees in tender green.

Sixth Child—

> June is bright with roses gay;
> Harebells bloom around her feet;

Seventh Child —

> Hot July rakes new mown hay
> From the meadows fresh and sweet.

Eighth Child—

> August's pleasant quiet reign
> Bids the meadow-lilies come;

Ninth Child—

> And September's golden grain
> Makes a welcome harvest home.

Tenth Child—

> Glad October's shining sun
> Paints the leaves in richest dyes;

Eleventh Child— .

> And November, dreary one,
> Shoots his arrows as he flies.

Twelfth Child—

> Cold December's latest breath
>   Makes the woods and meadows drear;
> And his eyelids close in death,
>   As he ends the happy year.

Poetry and Pictures.   —*Dora Read Goodale.*

A LIE.

> First somebody told it,
> Then the room wouldn't hold it,
> So the busy tongues rolled it
> Till they got it outside.
> Then the crowd came across it,
> And never once lost it,
> But tossed it and tossed it,
> Till it grew long and wide.

—*Old Rhyme.*

NOW.

> Waste not moments, no, nor words,
> In telling what you could do
> Some other time; the present is
> For doing what you should do.

—*Phoebe Cary.*

DISCONTENT.

[For Concert Recitation.]

> Down in a field, one day in June,
>   The flowers all bloomed together,
> Save one who tried to hide herself
>   And drooped, that pleasant weather.

> A robin, who had soared too high
>   And felt a little lazy,
> Was resting near a buttercup,
>   Who wished she were a daisy.

For daisies grow so trig and tall,
   She always had a passion
For wearing frills about her neck,
   Just in the daisies' fashion.

And buttercups must always be
   The same old tiresome color,
While daisies dress in gold and white,
   Although the gold is duller.

"Dear Robin," said this sad young flower,
   "Perhaps you'd not mind trying
To find a nice white frill for me,
   Some day when you are flying."

"You silly thing!" the robin said,
   "I think you must be crazy;
I'd rather be my honest self,
   Than any made-up daisy.

"You're nicer in your own bright gown;
   The little children love you;
Be the best buttercup you can,
   And think no flower above you.

"Though swallows keep me out of sight,
   We'd better keep our places;
Perhaps the world would all go wrong
   With one too many daisies.

"Look bravely up into the sky,
   And be content with knowing
That God wished for a buttercup
   Just here where you are growing."
                  —*Sarah O. Jewett.*

A SPRING STORY.

[*For Concert Recitation.*]

A Lady-bug and a Bumble-bee
Went out in the fine spring weather;
They met by chance on a lilac bush,
And talked for a while together.

6

"These days are warm," said the Bumble-bee,
"But the nights are damp and chilly;"
"So damp, indeed," said the Lady-bug,
"I should think you'd rent the Lily.

"I know it's '*To Let*,' I've seen the sign,
But it won't be long untaken;
The wonder is that so sweet a place
Should ever have been forsaken."

"A thousand thanks," said the Bee in haste,
"And if you'll excuse my hurry,
I'll go and secure the house at once,
Before there's a rush and flurry."

So off he flew towards Marigold street,—
(The way was not long nor hilly,)
But just as he passed the Pinks, he saw
A little girl pick the Lily,—

The only house he could find to rent,—
And this is the pitiful reason,
Why out on a cold, bare clover leaf
He slept the rest of the season.

You call this story too sad to tell—
Perhaps it is; but it teaches
A little rule to the little heart
Of each little girl it reaches.

And the rule is this: When springtime comes,
And the nights are damp and chilly,
Be very sure that it's not "*To Let*"
Before you gather a lily.

—Kate Kellogg.

UP AND DOWN.

When Billy Bolus wanted to ride,
And down on a rainbow's edge to slide,
He jumped so high and he jumped so far,
That he caught on the point of a little star;

And there he hung till a lark came by,
Who picked the hook of his frock from the eye,
And down to the earth the little boy fell,
Right into the mouth of a very deep well,
And dropped in a pail that was coming up,
And so he was carried away to the top.
When Billy was safe, he said that he guessed
He had better go home and take some rest.

Cat's Cradle.   *—Ed. Willett.*

OBEDIENCE.

If you're told to do a thing,
   And mean to do it really,
Never let it be by halves;
   Do it fully, freely.

Do not make a poor excuse,
   Waiting, weak, unsteady;
All obedience worth the name,
   Must be prompt and ready.

                       —Phoebe Cary.

THE WIND.

Which way does the wind blow,
   And where does he go?
He rides over the water,
   And over the snow.

O'er wood and o'er valley,
   And over the height,
Where goats cannot traverse,
   He taketh his flight.

He rages and tosses
   When bare is the tree,
As when you look upward,
   You plainly may see.

But whither he cometh,
   Or whither he goes,

There's no one can tell you—
There's no one who knows.

—Christina Rossetti.

THE SPRING WIND.

O wind, where have you been
That you smell so sweet?
Among the violets
Which bloom at your feet.

The honeysuckle waits
For Summer and for heat,
But violets in the chilly Spring
Make the turf so sweet.

—Christina Rossetti.

THE WIND AND THE MOON.
[*For Concert Recitation.*]

Said the Wind to the Moon, "I will blow you out.
　　You stare in the air
　　Like a ghost in a chair;
Always looking what I am about;
I hate to be watched; I will blow out."

The Wind blew hard, and out went the Moon.
　　So, deep, on a heap
　　Of clouds, to sleep.
Down lay the Wind, and slumbered soon—
Muttering low, "I've done for that Moon!"

He turned in his bed; she was there again!
　　On high in the sky,
　　With her one ghost eye,
The Moon shone white and alive and plain.
Said the Wind, "I will blow you out again."

The Wind blew hard, and the Moon grew dim.
　　"With my sledge and my wedge
　　I have knocked off her edge!
If I only blow right fierce and grim
The creature will soon be dimmer than dim."

He blew and he blew, and she thinned to a thread.
"One puff more's enough
To blow her to snuff!
One good puff more where the last was bred,
And glimmer, glimmer, glum, will go the thread!"

He blew a great blast and the thread was gone,
In the air, nowhere
Was a moonbeam bare;
Far off and harmless the shy stars shone:
Sure and certain the moon was gone.

The Wind, he took to his revels once more;
On down, in town,
Like a merry, mad clown,
He leaped and hallooed with whistle and roar,—
"What's that?" The glimmering thread once more!

He flew in a rage, he danced and blew;
But in vain was the pain
Of his bursting brain;
For still the broader the moon scrap grew,
The broader he swelled his big cheeks and blew.

Slowly she grew—till she filled the night,
And shone on her throne
In the sky alone,
A matchless, wonderful, silvery light,
Radiant and lovely, the queen of the night.

Said the Wind, " What a marvel of power am I,
With my breath, good faith!
I blew her to death—
First blew her away right out of the sky,
Then blew her in; what a strength am I !"

But the Moon she knew nothing about the affair,
For high in the sky,
With her one white eye,
Motionless, miles above the air,
She had never heard the great Wind blare.
—*Geo. MacDonald.*

THE DAYS OF THE WEEK.

A KITCHEN-GARDEN EXERCISE FOR SEVEN LITTLE GIRLS.

[Each character must wear a crown bearing the name of the day she represents: the one for SUNDAY being larger and handsomer than the others.]

MONDAY [*carrying a wash-board*]:

 I am a very busy day,
  I am just after Sunday;
 But many people slander me,
  And say I am blue Monday.
 I play upon an instrument,
  If every one would use—
   The wash-board good—
   They never would
 Be troubled with the blues.

TUESDAY [*carrying an ironing-board*]:

 Good-evening, sister, here I am,
  And I have work to do;
 For, though the clothes are nicely washed,
  They must be ironed, too.
 I starch and iron everything,
  And put them all away.
   So you will see
   That I must be
 A very busy day.

WEDNESDAY [*carrying a rolling-pin*]:

 Dear me, I have so much to do!
  I must be on my feet.
 Though clothes are washed, and ironed, too,
  They're never fit to eat.
 I make the bread, the cake, the pies,
  Doughnuts and cookies, too;
   With flour and spice,
   And all things nice,
 I work as well as you.

THURSDAY [*carrying knitting or sewing*]:

 There's something left for me to do,
  Which I will never shirk.

> I cut and fit,
> And sew and knit,
> Such is my daily work.
> What children wear
> They often tear;
> When other work is through,
> With thimble, thread,
> And needle bright,
> I make them good as new.

FRIDAY [*carrying a broom*]:

> Some call me an unlucky day;
> I don't know why they should,
> When oft they turn around and say
> That I am Friday Good.
> I wipe the doors
> And sweep the floors,
> The house I overhaul,
> To pave the way
> For Saturday, the busiest of all.

SATURDAY [*carrying wooden pail and scrubbing-brush*]:

> I an the biggest work-day,
> I make things splash and splatter,
> With scour and scrub,
> And rub-a-dub,
> On floor and tin and platter.
> But I must make things nice and clean
> For our dear sister-guest,
> The Sabbath day, of all the rest
> The sweetest and the best.

SUNDAY [*carrying an open Bible, passes slowly before all the days, beginning with Saturday, and then stands at the head beside Monday*]:

> My sisters, dear, you all are here,
> Each in your proper space.
> The last shall yet be first, you know,
> And so I take my place.
> On Sabbath day

No work or play
    Should lure us from the duty
        Of serving Him who made this earth,
    So full of life and beauty.

Journal Education.   —*Mattie McCaslin.*

GRACE AND THE MOON.

Dear little Grace at the window stood
    Watching that winter night
The great round moon in the far blue sky,
    Where it shown so big and bright,

Till a cloud swept over its shining face,
    Then she turned with a little pout;
"I wanted to look at the moon," she said,
    "But somebody's blowed it out!"

Wide Awake.   —*Brenda Aubert.*

WHERE ARE THE STARS?

"What ails the stars of heaven above,
    This dark and stormy night?"
Said Rosy Lee to Johnny Love,
    "They do not come in sight.

"Right by this window I have stood,
    From eight to half-past nine;
O, dear, I wish—I wish they would
    For one wee moment shine.

"I guess, I know the reason why,
    We cannot see them, Rose;
They've hid themselves away on high,
    The rain might soil their clothes.

"The moon is hiding with them,
    She does not show her face;
O, see, look, she is coming through,
    The clouds she tries to chase."

Like flocks of sheep they pass away,
  The twinkling stars come out;
They wink and nod and seem to say,
  "We know what we're about."

School and Home.   —*Minneola Rustic.*

THE PINE TREE ACADEMY.
[*For Concert Recitation.*]

All the birdies went to school,
In a pine tree, dark and cool,
At its foot a brook was flowing.
    The teacher was a crow
    And what he did not know,
You may be sure was not worth knowing.

Their satchels are hanging up tidy and neat,
They smooth down their feathers and wipe their feet.
While the wind through the tree-tops goes creeping.
    "Speak up loud," says the crow
    "I can't hear, as you know,
While the branches are swaying and creaking."

They are taught the very best way to fly,
To catch the insect that goes buzzing by,
How to cock the head when beginning to sing.
    "I've a cold," says the crow,
    "Or else I would show,
How the nightingale does when she makes the woods ring."

The books are made of maple leaves,
For paper, bark from white birch trees,
And for pencil each uses a stick.
    " When you write," says the crow,
    "Be both careful and slow,
"Make your letters look graceful, not thick."

Every birdie builds a nest,
In a place each thinks the best,
While the teacher gives good sound advice.

" All the stalks," says the crow,
" You must lay in a row,
Before using one, look at it twice."

All at once, with a cold blast
The rain comes falling, thick and fast,
While the old pine tree groans in the gale.
  "School is closed," says the crow,
  " You must all quickly go,
But to-morrow come back without fail."

—*V. E. Scharff.*

MISS LILYWHITE'S PARTY.

" May I go to Miss Lilywhite's party?"
  But grandmamma shook her head:
    " When the birds go to rest,
    I think it is best
  For mine to go too," she said.

" *Can't* I go to Miss Lilywhite's party?"
  Still grandmamma shook her head:
    "Dear child, tell me how,
    You're half-asleep now;
  Don't ask such a thing," she said.

Then that little one's laughter grew hearty.
  " Why, granny," she said,
" Going to Miss Lilywhite's party
  Means going to bed!"

—*St. Nicholas.*

THE SEASONS.

First Child—

  How I love the blooming Spring,
  When the birds so gaily sing!

Second Child—

  More the Summer me delights,
  With its lovely days and nights.

Third Child—

> Autumn is the best of all,
> With its fruits for great and small.

Fourth Child—

> Nay! old Winter is the time!
> Jolly then the sleighbells' chime!

Fifth Child, to the Others—

> Every season will be bright,
> Children, if you live aright.
>
> *—Picture Gallery.*

BEST OF THE DOLLIES.

Which of my dollies do I love best?
That is Miss Georgia Geneva West.
Look at her collar—Valenciennes lace!
She is a duchess, they call her " Your Grace!"

Her jewels are diamonds.   Papa calls them paste.
Oh, she's got up in such exquisite taste!
But Miss Georgia Anna Geneva West,
You are not the dolly that I love best.

This is the handsomest dolly of all;
See, she's all dressed for the great fancy ball!
Her dress is real satin; just feel it and see.
Aunt sent her from Paris on purpose for me.

Real jet black hair, with a bandeau of pearls;
Don't they look beautiful over her curls?
I know that my favorite you think you have guessed,
But she's not the one that I love the best.

This is the china baby doll;
Don't you think she's the sweetest of all?
Bright blue eyes, and the rosiest lips;
She wears the cunningest baby slips.

Muslin clear-starched, with a beautiful gloss,
Pink coral necklace, anchor and cross.
Oh, she's the daintiest, darlingest pet,
But there's another I love better yet.

Where is black Topsy—the old woolen doll?
Out on the pavement where Bess let her fall,
Out of the fifth-story window, I think,
But then it won't hurt her; she don't even wink.

She's dressed in green calico apron and cap,
She never gets broken, nor cares for a rap,
She is my comfort above all the rest;
And really and truly *I love her the best.*

—Kate Allyn.

THE LETTER.

Did you ever get a letter?
  I did, the other day;
It was in a real envelope,
  And it came a long, long way.

A stamp was in the corner,
  And some printing, when it came;
And the one that wrote the letter
  Had put "Miss" before my name.

Then there came a lot more writin'—
  I forget now what it read,
But it told the office people
  Where I lived, my mamma said.

Don't you suppose those letter people,
  If they hadn't just been told,
Would have thought 'twas for a lady
  Who was awful, awful old?

For it looked real big and heavy;
  The outside was stuck with glue,

So they couldn't know I'm little—
I don't think they could, do you?
                    —*Primary Fridays.*

WON'T AND WILL.

Sha'n't and Won't were two little brothers,
    Angry and sullen and gruff;
Try and Will are dear little sisters,
    One can scarcely love them enough.

Sha'n't and Won't looked down at their noses,
    Their faces were dismal to see;
Try and Will are brighter than roses
    In June, and as blithe as a bee.

Sha'n't and Won't are backward and stupid,
    Little, indeed, did they know;
Try and Will learn something new daily,
    And seldom are heedless or slow,

Sha'n't and Won't came to terrible trouble;
    Their story is awful to tell;
Try and Will are in the school-room,
    Learning to read and to spell.

THE CONCEITED GRASSHOPPER.

There was a little grasshopper
Forever on the jump;
And, as he never looked ahead,
He often got a bump.

His mother said to him one day,
As they were in the stubble,
"If you don't look before you leap,
You'll get yourself in trouble."

The silly little grasshopper
Despised his wise old mother

And said he knew what best to do,
And bade her not to bother.

He hurried off across the fields—
An unknown path he took—
When, oh! he gave a heedless jump,
And landed in the brook.

He struggled hard to reach the bank—
A floating straw he seizes—
When quick a hungry trout darts out,
And tears him all to pieces.

SWEET PEAS.

Once within my garden wall,
  From their daily flight,
Rested a flock of butterflies,
  All in pink and white.

Why they chose my garden plot
  I shall never know—
But people call them now sweet peas,
  And really think they grow!

St. Nicholas.   *—Mildred Howells.*

A MORNING WALK.

[A boy, riding a long stick, takes off his hat and bows to two ladies, in street costumes, with dolls in arms and in carriages.]

Boy—Good morning, ladies. Is not this beautiful weather? I hope that both yourselves and the children are well.

First Girl—O, yes, indeed! We are just taking our youngest children out to get the fresh morning air in the park.

Second Girl—My six children have all been ill with the mumps, and I have been worried to death about them.

Boy—Look out for mad dogs.

Girls [*scream and run*]—O, O, O, where? where? where?

Boy—I did not say there was one around here, but there *might* be, and it is best to be careful.

Second Girl—O, pray, don't frighten us so again!

First Girl—That is a fine horse that you are riding. Aren't you afraid that he will throw you off?

Boy—Hm, hm, no, no. *I* can ride *any* horse [*horse prances*], but you ought to keep away from this one's heels, as he always kicks. [*Turns the horse's heels towards the girls, and kicks in a lively manner.*]

Girls—O, keep him still, keep him still! do, do, keep him still!

Boy—He is a very gay young horse, and does not like to stand still. Won't you get on him and take a ride? Splendid exercise!

First Girl—No, indeed! *I prefer* to walk any day.

Second Girl—We have talked too long. I am afraid the children are getting cold. [*Doll cries.*] Baby is crying. Sh, sh!

First Girl—I am getting quite hungry. [*Consults watch.*] Why, it is almost lunch time!

Girls—Good-day!

Boy [*bowing*]—Ladies, look out for mice!

Girls [*gathering up their skirts and running*]—Mice? run! run!   —*Helen W. Boyden.*

SPEAK THE TRUTH.

Speak the truth!
Speak it boldly, never fear;
Speak it so that all may hear;
In the end it shall appear
Truth is best in age or youth.
Always, always speak the truth!

THE WONDERFUL BEAN-VINE.

Billy Bogardus planted a bean-vine,
Which grew so fast in a night,
That, when he got up in the morning,
The top was far out of sight.

He made a balloon,
And sailed to the moon,
But there was the bean-vine just as soon.

The man in the moon was so cranky,
That he ate the beans as fast as they grew,
And he never stopped to boil or to stew,
And never once said, "Thank ye."

Then Billy came down and put on his boots,
And pulled the bean-vine up by the roots,
And said, "It grew well for a night in June,
But *I* plant *no beans* for the man in the moon."

Cat's Cradle.   —*Edward Willett.*

KEEP PUSHING.

Keep pushing! 'tis wiser than stepping aside,
And sighing and watching and waiting the tide;
In life's earnest battle they only prevail,
Who daily march onward and never say fail.

SIT STILL.

[Little girl arranges several dolls in a row. Paper ones will do.]

Now, every one of you children,
 [*raises her finger*]
Sit still against the pane,
And do not stir from out your place
Till I come back again.

I am going into the garden
To see if the currants are red,
And, after you've had your supper
I'll put you all to bed.

            —*Easy Book.*

TWO ROBINS.

Robin Gray is a black-eyed boy,
Fond of goodies and every toy.
Robin Red is a black-eyed bird—
Sauciest Bob one ever heard.

Good Robin Gray says: "If you please,"
Bonniest boy one often sees.
Bad Robin Red steals cherries all,
And don't say "Thank you," when you call.

Robin Gray cares for blue-eyed dolls,
Horses and carts and bouncing balls.
Robin Red cares for babies four
Just peeping out at tree-top door.

UNAPPRECIATED.

[Two boys, one with a book, meet at the middle of platform.]

First—I have just written a book of poetry. Stop a moment while I read a few stanzas from my favorites [*Friend listens scowling. Reads pathetically*]:

"Old Mother Hubbard
Went to the cup-board
To get her poor dog—"

Second [*interrupting*]—Why, *that* is genuine doggerel!
First—I did not expect *you* to understand a true classic. You are not educated up to it. Listen to this gem [*Reads lightly*]:

"A cat came fiddling out of a barn—"

I suppose you call *that* catterel!
Second—It is quite musical, I assure you. Any more?
First—Here's my favorite [*tragically*]:

"Three children sliding on the ice,
Upon a summer's day;
It so fell out, they all fell in—"

7

Second—Suppose they were *my* children! [*Runs off.*]

First [*looking after him*]—That's just the way everyone runs away whenever I read one of *my* poems to them. I don't see *why!*

—Helen W. Boyden.

JOHNNY CAKE.

[Provide the children with the articles mentioned in the stanzas.]

First Child—

>This is the seed
>So yellow and round
That little John Horner hid in the ground

Second Child—

>These are the leaves
>So graceful and tall
That grew from the seed so yellow and small.

Third Child—

>This is the stalk
>That came up between
The leaves so pretty and graceful and green.

Fourth Child—

>These are the tassels
>So flowery, that crowned
The stalk so smooth, so strong and so round.

Fifth Child—

>These are the husks
>With satin inlaid
That grew 'neath the tassels that drooped and swayed.

Sixth Child—

>This is the silk
>In shining threads spun
A treasure it hides from the frost and the sun.

Seventh Child—

>This is the treasure—
>Corn, yellow as gold—
That satin and silk so softly unfold.

Eighth Child—
> This is the cake
> For Johnny to eat—
> Made from the corn, so yellow and sweet.
>> *—Easy Book.*

PANSIES.

The dear little pansies are lifting their heads,
    All purple and blue and gold;
They are cov'ring with beauty the dark garden beds,
    And hiding from sight the dark mold.

The dear little pansies, they nod and they smile,
    Their faces upturned to the sky;
"We are trying to make the world pretty and bright,"
    They whisper to each passer by.

Now all little children who try every day
    Kind-hearted and loving to be,
Are helping the pansies to make the world bright
    And beautiful; don't you see?
>> *—Ruth Wilson.*

MOTHER'S EYES.

I guess God made my mamma's eyes
With some of the blue that's in the skies,
For when I look into them I see
Two little angels looking at me.

Congregationalist.   *— W. B. Seabrook.*

THE SHADOW.

I have a little shadow that goes in and out with me,
And what can be the use of him is more than I can see.
He is very, very like me, from the heels up to the head;
And I see him jump before me when I jump into my bed.

The funniest thing about him is the way he likes to grow,
Not at all like proper children, which is always very slow;
For he sometimes shoots up taller like an india-rubber ball,
And he sometimes gets so. little that there's none of him at all.

He hasn't got a notion of how children ought to play,
And can only make a fool of me in every sort of way,
He stays so close beside me, he's a coward you can see;
I'd think shame to stick to nursie as that shadow sticks to me!

One morning, very early, before the sun was up,
I rose and found the shining dew on every buttercup;
But my lazy little shadow, like an arrant sleepy head,
Had stayed at home behind me and was fast asleep in bed.

—R. L. Stevenson.

THE DANDELION.

I am a bold fellow
   As ever was seen,
With my shield of yellow
   In the grass of green.

You may uproot me
   From field and from lane,
Trample me, cull me—
   I spring up again.

I never flinch, sir,
   Wherever I dwell;
Give me an inch, sir,
   I'll soon take an ell.

Drive me from garden
   In anger and pride,
I'll thrive and harden
   By the road-side.

—Dinah Mulock Craik.

WHAT A CHILD MAY HAVE.

A little child may have a loving heart
    Most dear and sweet,
    And willing feet.

A little child may have a gentle voice
    And pleasant tongue
    For every one.

IF.

First Boy–
    O, if I only had a pair
    Of Indian snow-shoes I could wear—
    The storms might beat, the winds might blow,
    Across the drifts I'd northward go,

Second Boy—
    And if·I only had a boat
    I'd spread my sail and eastward float,
    And see the far off Eastern lands;
    The palm trees and the desert lands.

Third Boy—
    And if I only had a horse
    I'd westward, westward take my course
    With flying feet and floating mane
    He'd gallop with me o'er the plain.

Fourth Boy—
    And if I had some wings to fly
    I'd southward soar along the sky
    And see the Southland all aglow
    With roses when with us there's snow.

Girl—
    O, if you want to and you can,
    I'm willing you should roam;
    But I'm dear Mother's girl,
    I'll stay with her at home.

—Easy Book.

VACATION.

A little Girl—

> Boys and girls of every nation,
> High and low of every station,
> Sing your sweetest songs again,
> Shout aloud the glad refrain,
> For vacation time is here,
> Gladdest day of all the year.

First Boy—

> O, out in the orchard this morning
> A robin so loud, and so clear,
> Was calling to me, " Wake up, little boy!
> Don't you know vacation is here?"

First Girl—

> And when I was down in the meadow
> The flowers, so sweet and so gay,
> Were nodding, and beck'ning, and whisp'ring,
> "Vacation is coming to-day."

Second Boy—

> O, hark! how the bees are all buzzing,
> Each insect with low, drowsy humming,
> The grass and the breeze, the leaves o' the trees,

All—

> All tell us vacation is coming.

Third Boy—

> Yes, glad vacation is coming,
> Old school-time, you've had your day,
> Through all the year we have studied well,
> And now is the time for play.

Large Girl [represents teacher]—

> And what will you do in vacation,
> My glad little girl and boy?
> Don't you know the saying, "All play and no work
> Makes Jack but a useless toy?"

First Boy—

> What will I do? O, plenty of things,
> I'll walk, I'll run, and I'll ride,

Go sailing, and hunting and fishing,
And thousands of things beside.

Large Girl—

And you, my lass?

First Girl—

I'll play with my doll,
And I'll run in the meadow too.
O, I know the day will be all too short,
For all I shall have to do.

Large Girl—

And so you will play all the summer?

All—

Yes, just like the butterflies.

Large Girl—

But don't you know, when the winter comes,
Each butterfly *shivers* and *dies?*

He has laid up no store of honey,
There is nothing for him to eat,
And the first chill breath of the icy blast
Stretches him dead at your feet.

Nay, be like the bees, my children,
And not like the butterflies gay,
Bees' lives are spent 'mong the flowers,
They mingle their *work* with their play.

Let *kind deeds, pleasant words*, be the honey
You store for your friends each year,
If you only go seeking for *pleasure*,
They'll be sorry vacation is here.

Don't be idle, or cross and selfish,
Because you are out of school,
Play like the *lambs*, and *sing* like the *birds*,
But remember the *Golden Rule*.

School—Do unto others as you would have them do unto
you.

First little Girl—

We'll remember the Golden Rule,
And we'll try to follow it too,
We mean to grow wiser, but best of all,
We are going to be honest and true.

   [*Turns to audience*]

And now here's a welcome to all
Our friends, and a hearty cheer.
We are glad you have come to see us,
And to hear what we've done through the year.

All school sing—

   [Tune: MARCHING THROUGH GEORGIA.]

Glad vacation's coming, boys,
It's coming here to-day,
Give it now a welcome,
For it's coming quick this way.
Give it three times three, my laddies,
All hurrah! we say.
Run then to sea-side and mountains,
Hurrah! Hurrah!
We sing vacation's day,
Hurrah! Hurrah!
The time has come to play,
So we sing vacation,
All so merry, blithe and gay.
Run then to sea-side and mountains.

—Lizzie M. Hadley.

LITTLE THINGS.

[*Speech for a Little Boy.*]

A little theft, a small deceit,
   Too often leads to more;
'Tis hard at first, but tempts the feet
   As through an open door.
Just as the broadest rivers run
   From small and distant springs,
The greatest crimes that men have done
   Have grown from little things.

IN MY POCKET.

Yes, I have it in my pocket;
But nobody put it there.
If you take it from my pocket,
It will not be anywhere.

Curious thing this in my pocket.
Something add. it's smaller still;
Yet you can by adding nothing
Make it larger if you will.

Funny thing this in my pocket,
Holding there its given space:
If you like, a second something
Easily fills the self-same place.

This odd thing within my pocket,
Just its like was never seen,
Yet a hundred million billion
Of its kind have often been.

This queer thing within my pocket
(Don't tell any living soul;
It's a great, a wondrous secret):
This strange thing is just—a hole!

PHIL AND MAUDE.

[Little girl, with school bag, meets small boy. Both wear hats.]

Boy—Where are you going, little Miss, so early in the morning?

Girl—I am going to school. Didn't you know that I had been to school for 'most a week?

Boy [*contemptuously*]—Why, you are not big enough!

Girl—I am 'most as big as *you* are, and I am six years old too.

Boy—What do you do in school—play?

Girl [*indignantly*]—No, indeed! I read and write, and do examples in 'rithmetic.

Boy—Well, how much are three and five?

Girl [*trying to count on her fingers*]—Three and five?
three— three— three and— and five are— three and five—
hm; why, six, of course.

Boy [*scornfully*]—O, O, why, *everybody* knows that three
and five are fifteen!

Girl—If you knew, what did you ask me for then?

Boy—How smart you are! Can you read any better than
you can do examples?

Girl—I've read my book through 'most a hundred times.
I can read it bottom upwards, and even with the covers shut.
Can *you* do *that?*

Boy—Of course, I can. What a silly question! Let me
see your writing.

Girl—I guess I've lost my pencil, and I haven't time to
stay and answer any more of *your* silly questions anyway.
The bell will ring in a minute, and I do not wish to be late.

—*Helen W. Boyden.*

A BIT OF ADVICE.

Little children, you must seek
Rather to be good than wise,
The thoughts you do not speak
Shine out in your face and eyes.

—*Alice Cary.*

TRUANTS.

When the sun was tired and slipped behind a cloud,
All the little rain-drops gathered in a crowd,
Whispering together, "*He* will never know,
Let us take a holiday, let us fall below."

When the sun was rested and wandered out, he found
All the little rain-drops fallen to the ground.
" Well," he thought, " I'm sorry, but I'll try to smile,
That will bring them back again in a little while."

MY KINDERGARTEN

[Have a little girl arrange her dolls—paper ones will do—in a row, and then introduce them as follows:]

This is my class.
I am teacher you see;
They stand in a row
And listen to me;
And never once
Have I seen them try
To whisper or laugh;
They are very shy.

I sometimes fear
They will never do
The nice little games
When I ask them to:
To keep good time
To march and sing,
And whirl about
In a pretty ring.

—*Mrs. S. J. Brigham.*

NEVER MIND.

First Small Girl—

O, dear! I can't go out to-day,
Because it's raining so.

Large Girl—

Never mind, never mind!
'Twill make the garden grow.
If rain should always go away,
Whenever children ask it,
We'd never gather beans enough
To fill a little basket.

Second Small Girl—

O, dear! I cannot work to-day,
The sun is shining so.

Large Girl—

Never mind, never mind!
'Twill make the flowers grow;
For if the sun would cease to shine
Whenever folks complain
We'd never have it warm enough
To ripe the fields of grain.

Third Small Girl—

O, dear! I cannot walk to-day,
So strong the wind doth blow.

Large Girl—

Never mind, never mind!
'Twill make the mill sails go.
If all at once the wind should drop
To please such folks as we,
What would become of all the ships
That sail upon the sea!

—*Agnes M. Claussen.*

WHAT WE BELIEVE.

First Boy—

Don't tell me of to-morrow,
  Give me the boy who'll say
That when a good deed's to be done,
  "Let's do the deed to-day."

Second Boy—

The fisher who draws in his net too soon,
  Won't have any fish to sell.
The child who shuts up his book too soon,
  Won't learn any lessons well.

Third Boy—

If a task is once begun
  Never leave it till it's done;
Be the labor great or small,
  Do it well or not at all.

SOME ADVICE.

Good-morrow, little rose-bush,
  I pray thee, tell me true,
To be as sweet as a sweet red rose
  What must a body do?

To be as sweet as a sweet red rose
  A little girl like you
Just grows and grows and grows and grows
  And that's what she must do.

THE BIRD'S BREAKFAST.

Two little birdies
  One winter day
Began to wonder,
  And then to say,
" How about breakfast,
  This wintry day? "

Two little maidens,
  One wintry day,
Into the garden
  Wended their way,
Where the snow lay deep
  That wintry day.

One with a broom
  Swept the snow away;
One scattered crumbs,
  Then away to play;
And birdies had breakfast
  That wintry day.

LITTLE THINGS.

Little moments make an hour;
  Little thoughts, a book;
Little seeds, a tree or flower;

Water-drops, a brook;
Little deeds of faith and love,
Make a home for you above.

THE NEWS.

[Two boys coming from opposite directions meet on platform.]

First Gentleman —Good morning, what's the news?

Second Gentleman —Really, I don't know.   I have had no time to read this morning.   Mother-in-law is visiting with us.

Newsboy (with armful of papers passes).—Mornin' News, yer's your Mornin' News.

First Gentleman —Here, boy, I'll take one.   (*buys paper, opens and reads*). Well, I declare! Wife always expected it!

Second Gentleman (eagerly) —What's that?

First Gentleman (looking up) —You remember the giddy Miss Dish who ran away with young Spoon?

Second Gentleman —Certainly; it was the season when milk was so high.   The affair was the talk of the town. • Have they parted?

First Gentleman —O, no! There has been a collision on the Pan Handle and she has sustained a fracture; Spoon is in a great stew over it and has sued the company.

Second Gentleman —Well, well!

First Gentleman (resumes his reading).—Listen (*reads aloud*) Our citizens will be pleased to learn that the Knave has been arrested with all the tarts—

Second Gentleman (excitedly) —Where?

First Gentleman —Right here in Chicago.

Second Gentleman —The tarts must be well jammed by this time.

First Gentleman (continuing to read to himself, suddenly exclaims) —Old Grimes has failed!

Second Gentleman —You don't say so!   What's the trouble?

First Gentleman (as he folds his paper) —Short on breath.

Second Gentleman —You astonish me.   I am interested in that myself.   Let us investigate.

(*Walk off together.*)   —*Helen W. Boyden.*

A LITTLE ONE'S WELCOME.

Welcome, daisies, from your sleep!
 Snow has left the ground,—
Winter's gone; you need not peep
 So timidly around!

Welcome, pale green vale and hill,
 Homes of bird and bee!
You, too, silver splashing rill,
 That used to talk to me.

Welcome, buds upon the bough
 Drooping o'er the eves!
Tho' you're only babies now.
 You'll soon be grown-up leaves.

Welcome, soft, blue, sunny sky,
 Birds and blossoms gay!
Now you've come at last to try
 A good long while to stay.

LITTLE JOHNNIE JUMP-UP.

Little Johnnie Jump-up was hiding in some mold,
Away from old winter, whose fingers are so cold
That little Johnnie sobbed to a mole that was by:
" If winter should touch me I shall die, I shall die."
Winter did not find him, and when 'twas spring weather
The mole and Johnnie came creeping out together.
The mole was soon burrowing in search of drink and food,
And left our little hero all alone in the wood.
Jump-up was not idle.   Every day, every hour,
He drank the rich mold-wine, and grew a handsome flower.
He wore a blue jacket and a sweet breath he had.
Is it a wonder that the maiden's heart was glad,
When walking in the woodland she espied one day
Little Johnnie Jump-up and carried him away?
                                        —*Kit McKean.*

THREE THOUGHTS FOR THREE BOYS.

First Boy—

Better for a man to possess manners than beauty, wealth or talent; they will more than supply all.

Second Boy—

Politeness is to do or say
The kindest things in the kindest way.

Third Boy—

Count as lost that day in which you have done no good. It is better to be nobly remembered than nobly born.

LITTLE SOLDIERS.

Be brave little soldiers,
To battle for right;
Before and behind you
The foe is in sight.

Beware of pitfalls
In paths yet untrod;
Be true to your manhood,
And so to your God.

You need for your weapons
A heart that is pure;
A will that is ready
To do and endure.

The enemy's crafty,
In league with all sin,
But the brave little soldier
The battle will win.   *—E. E Rexford.*

MY DOLLY.

[Little girl talking to her doll.]

Dolly Dimple,
Why so simple,

Why not sometimes look more staid?
      Have all dollies
      Thus your follies,
Is it 'cause you are afraid?
      You're so silly,
      Little Willy
Thinks you are a stupid maid!

      O, my dolly,
      Not your folly
That you're face's with smiles o'erlaid.
      I am sorry
      You should worry,
'Cause I did your smiles upbraid;
      Yes, my jolly
      Little dolly,
When I knew "it's the way you're made!"
                  —*E. M. B*

HARRY'S DOG.

Harry has a little dog—
Such a cunning fellow!
With a very shaggy coat,
Streaked with white and yellow.

Harry's dog has shining eyes,
And a nose so funny!
Harry wouldn't sell his dog
For a mint of money.

Harry's dog will never bark,
Never bite a stranger;
So he'd be of no account
Where there's any danger.

Harry has a little dog—
Such a cunning fellow!
But his dog is MADE OF WOOD,
Painted white and yellow.   —*Josephine Pollard.*

CHERRIES.

Round and red,
   Hanging together,
Ripening fast,
   In the summer weather.

Robin red-breast,
   Who asked you?
Do you think you ought
   To have some, too?

"They're all mine!"
   Says Redbreast Robin,
Eating away
   With his head a-bobbin'.

            —Mrs. M. F. Butts.

BIDDY AND HER EGG.

Wanted! wanted! everyone to know,
   Cackle! cackle! cut, cut, ka— da— cut!
I've laid an egg! just as white as snow!
   Cackle! cackle! cut, cut, ka— da— cut!

Just come and see it—lying in the nest—
   Cackle! cackle! cut, cut, ka— da— cut!
'Tis the biggest egg, the handsomest and best!
   Cackle! cackle! cut, cut, ka— da— cut!

Foolish Mrs. Biddy! have you never heard—
   Cackle! cackle! cut, cut, ka— da— cut!
Other hens lay eggs as well as you, my bird?
   Cackle! cackle! cut, cut, ka— da— cut!

When you do a thing you should not boast and swell—
   Cackle! cackle! cut, cut, ka— da— cut!
Let other people praise you and your merit tell.
   Cackle! cackle! cut, cut, ka— da— cut!

JEFFERSON'S TEN RULES.
[*For ten little children.*]

1. Never put off till to-morrow what you can do to-day.
2. Never trouble another for what you can do yourself.
3. Never spend your money before you have it.
4. Never buy what you do not want because it is cheap.
5. Pride costs us more than hunger, thirst and cold.
6. We seldom repent of having eaten too little.
7. Nothing is troublesome that we do willingly.
8. How much pain the evils have cost us that have never happened.
9. Take things always by the smooth handle.
10. When angry, count ten before you speak; if very angry, count a hundred.

BUZZ, BUZZ.
[Little girl with doll.]

Buzz, buzz, little black fly,
No, to hurt you I'll not try;
Dolly and I will love you too;
You'll love me and and I'll love you.
Don't you come to dolly's face, please;
Don't you tickle my nose and tease;
Dolly will love you then, and I
Never will hurt you, little black fly.
Don't go yet, you dearest of things;
Dolly is seeing you wash your wings;
Dolly is washed and sometimes cries:
You wash yourself, you best of flies.
Do that again, black fly, we beg;
Comb your hair with your small black leg.
So you are going? well, good-by;
Come again soon, please, dear black fly.

ONE BY ONE.

One step and then another,
And the longest walk is ended;

One stitch and then another,
And the longest rent is mended;
One brick upon another,
And the highest wall is made;
One flake upon another,
And the deepest snow is laid.

THE PEDDLER.

[*A Street Scene.*]

[Peddler with basket; gentleman with hat and cane.]

Gentleman [*bowing*]—How is business to-day?

Peddler [*wiping his eyes*]—Poor, very poor. I have a wife and ten children to support.

G. [*walking on*]—Too bad! too bad!

P. [*following and opening the basket*]—Won't you buy something? Handkerchiefs?

G.—O, O, hum, hum. No. I don't want anything. I would buy of you if I did.

P.—Here's a fine ribbon for your wife's hair. Only ten cents.

G. [*glancing at it*]—Sorry, but she wears a wig.

P.—Here's a doll for the baby—

G. [*crossly*]—Haven't any baby!

P.—Pity *me* then; I have ten sick with the mumps. Do buy this nice candy. I made it myself.

G. [*looking at candy*]—Well, I'll take *one* stick to help you along.

P.—Better take two; one for your wife.

G.—Can't afford it; candy isn't good for her [*gives him money*].

P. [*taking off his hat and bowing*]—Thank you, sir, thank you! —*Helen W. Boyden.*

A QUEER HOUSE.

There's a queer little house, and it stands in the sun;
When the good mother calls, in her children all run;
And while under her roof they are cosy and warm,
Tho' the wind it may whistle and bluster and storm.

Now the wee folks all mind there and indoors they keep,
Tho' out of the windows their tiny heads peep:
Would you see this queer house?   Go and watch the old hen
While her downy wings cover her chicks nine or ten;

—Geo. Cooper.

WHO I AM.

I'm my mamma's little darling,
Don't you think I'm fresh and sweet
With these roses on my shoulders
And my linen dress so neat?

Mamma made it just on purpose
'Cause I'se going to speak to you.
It is lovely!   Don't you think so?
Wish 'twas yours?   I'm sure you do.

GOD'S DIAMONDS.

See the sky, as darkness covers
Earth with sombre veil of night,
What a twinkling, blinking, winking,
Just like sparkling diamonds bright.

Ah! I know the names of many,
Know the place they stay at night;
Little stars, your worlds of brightness
Ever charm us with your light.

Said the moon in jealous anger
At the praise I did indite:
"Only just one moment wait you
See, then, how I'll dim their light."

But the peerless stars did twinkle,
Twinkle on in merry glee;
Looking shyly at the moonbeams,
As if saying, " Wait and see!"

—Mrs. Emily M. Boyden.

FRIGHTENED BIRDS.

"Hush! hush!" said the little brown thrush,
To her mate on the nest in the elder-brush.
"Keep still, don't open your bill!
There's a boy coming birdnesting over the hill. .
Let go your wings out so
That not an egg or the nest shall show.
Chee! chee! It seems to me
I'm as frightened as ever a bird can be."

Then still, with quivering bill,
They watched the boy out of sight o'er the hill.
Ah! then in the branches again,
Their glad song rang over hill and glen.
O, O, if that boy *could* know
How glad they were when they saw him go;
Say, say, do you think next day
He could possibly steal those eggs away?

MY MOTHER.

My mother, dearest mother!
  She loved me long ago;
There is, on earth, no other
  That ever loved me so.
I ought to try to please her
  And all her words to mind,
And never vex or tease her,
  Nor speak a word unkind.
              —*Every Child's Paper.*

MAY BABIES.

On the apple boughs little baby flowers
Are growing in the sun and the soft May showers.
On the meadow slopes baby violets, too,
Turn towards the sky their eyes of blue.

Just outside the door, I hear sweet robin-words,
All about a nest for some baby birds.
If you'll go with me you shall hear peep! peep!
See ten baby chickens going fast asleep.

And the best of all, little baby brother
With his eyes shut tight, nestles close to mother.
There are so many babies in house and field and tree
The world is just as full of joy as it can be.

SPEECH.
[*For a Small Boy.*]

They thought I couldn't make a speech
    I'm such a little tot!
I'll show them whether I can do
    A thing or two or not.

Don't be afraid to fight the Wrong,
    Or stand up for the Right;
And when you've nothing else to say,
    Be sure you say—Good-night.

THE NEST.

Blue-bird, bonny blue-bird, up in a tree,
Show me your speckled eggs, one, two, three;
Why do you hide them under your breast?
Just let me peep in the little round nest.

Blue-bird laughed as she sat in her nest,
Hiding her pretty eggs under her breast;
One sunny morning up in a tree
Chirped the new birdies, one, two, three.

THE DARLING GIRL.
[*For Two Little Girls.*]

First—

Who's the darling little girl
    Every body loves to *see?*

Second—
>   She it is whose sunny face
>   Is as *sweet* as SWEET can be.

First—
>   Who's the darling little girl
>   *Every* body loves to *hear?*

Second—
>   She it is whose *pleasant* voice
>   Falls like *music* on the ear.

THE BOY WE NEED.

We need the boy who's not afraid
 To do his share of work;
Who never is by toil dismayed,
 And never tries to shirk.

The boy whose heart is brave to meet
 All lions in the way;
Who's not discouraged by defeat,
 But tries another day.

WE NEVER TALK SCANDAL.

[*A Home Scene.*]

[One girl sits reading, but closes the book as soon as her neighbor comes in. The latter has a shawl over her head.]

Mrs. A. (seating herself)—I thought I'd drop in to rest for a few minutes. Have you heard the latest news about Bopeep?

Mrs. C. (interestedly)—Why, no! Has she found her sheep?

Mrs. A.—Several days ago; but the careless girl—they say —went to sleep yesterday and some tramp cut off the tails of all her sheep.

Mrs. C.—Dreadful! What will they do without them!

Mrs. A.—It is scandalous! What is the world coming to!

Mrs. C.—It was only yesterday that dear old Mother

Hubbard was sent to the poor-house. Simple Simon said she was starving—actually starving! Very few of her neighbors feel sorry for her because she *would* keep that dog.

Mrs. A.—What a tale-bearer that Simple is! I don't see how Mrs. Simon can allow it. Why, when my son came home the other day and told me what had happened to old maid Betsy Pringle, I whipped him soundly and sent him to bed.

Mrs. C.—Why, was it not he that told how Tom Piper stole pigs?

Mrs. A. (rising) —It was his duty to warn the neighbors. There is quite a difference between scandalous tale-bearing and doing one's duty.

Mrs. C.—I always try to keep on the charitable side and say as little as possible. *—Helen W. Boyden.*

ONCE UPON A TIME.

Now, once upon a time, there were three children
    And each of them had little daisy crowns
Their mother freely wove for them each morning,
    And all of them wore dotted muslin gowns.

And, once upon a time, the three went rambling
    Away from home, amid the wild greenwood;
And, once upon a time, they met a lambkin,
    And not a wolf like poor Red Riding Hood.

And, once upon a time, the three fell weeping;
    "Oh, we are lost! Where can our mothers be?"
Then meekly spake the little snow-white lambkin:
    "If you will come, I'll take you home with me."

And, once upon a time, the lambkin trotted
    Briskly away (the west was turning gold),
And, once upon a time, the children followed,
    And entered shyly in the lambkin's fold.

And, once upon a time, among the lambkins
    The children slumbered, in their muslin gowns,
Till morning came, and then they found their mother,
    Who wove for them anew their daisy crowns.
                               — Wide Awake.

CHATTERBOX SPEAKS.

They call me little Chatterbox
　My name is little May.
I have to talk so much, because
　I have so much to say.
And, O, I have so many friends!
　So many, and, you see,
I can't help loving them because
　They, everyone, love me.
I love my papa and mamma;
　I love my sisters too;
And, if you're very, very good,
　I guess that I'll love you.

———

A CLOSING ADDRESS.

Kind friends and dear parents,
　We have welcomed you here,
To our schoolroom so pleasant,
　And teacher so dear;
We hope we have pleased you
　By what we have learned,
And proved that our hearts
　To our books have been turned.

But you must remember
　That we are quite small,
And what we have done,
　May not please you all.
Yet, since we have labored
　To give you our best,
Please commend what is good,
　And pass by the rest.

—Speaker and Songster.

———

OLD SHOES.

How much a man is like old shoes!
For instance, both a soul may lose;

Both have been tanned; both are made tight
By cobblers; both get left and right;
Both need a mate to be complete,
And both are made to go on feet.
They both need heeling, oft are sold,
And both in time all turn to mold.
With shoes the last is first; with men
The first shall be the last; and when
The shoes wear out they are men-dead, too.
They are trod upon, and both
Will tread on others, nothing loath.
Both have their ties, and both incline
When polished in the world to shine;
And both peg out—and would you choose
To be a man or be his shoes?

—Teacher.

"A DISTRACTED MOTHER."

[Concert Recitation for School.]

A nice little motherly hen was she,
And as proud of her chickens as she could be;
   Oh, they were a funny lot!
Their toes turned in and their bills were round,
And they always waddled over the ground
   In search of a muddy spot.

"Cluck, cluck!" would the mother-hen loudly call,
As soon as the rain began to fall;
   "Come in, my dears, you'll get wet!"
"Quack, quack! Quack, quack!" said the ducklings four;
"Cluck, cluck!" said the hen, "don't you see it pour?"
   "Quack, quack!" they answered, "not yet!"

Though hard she scratched with her willing feet,
She couldn't get them enough to eat—
   The horribly greedy things!
And they didn't seem to have any sense;
For they wouldn't roost on the barn-yard fence,
   Or make any use of their wings.

As they grew older, the mother-hen
Went out with her chickens a-walking, when
    They came to a pretty pond;
And into it straight, with a fearless dash,
The web-footed chickens went splashety-splash,
    And scared their mother so fond—
Scared her verily out of her wits,
Into spasms and fainting fits;
    She still kept crying: " Cluck, cluck.
You'll drown! You'll drown! my dear quartet!"
"Oh, no, we won't; you needn't fret!"
    Exclaimed each naughty duck.

As they grew bigger, they wouldn't mind,
But wandered off wherever inclined,
    And the motherly hen declared
That, if they continued behaving so,
She wasn't to blame, and they might go
    And drown, for all that she cared.

The Nursery.   *—Josephine Pollard.*

THE CHILD AND THE RAINBOW.

Little Child (at Mother's knee)—

    O, Mother! do you see the sky
      With lines of red and gold?
    O, see! how closely they do lie
      In blue and purple fold!

    What is it, Mother? how it bends!
      So beautiful it glows
    With colors, rich in beauty, blends;
      I wonder if God knows?

    O, tell me, Mother, why 'tis so;
      If God will let it fall
    Where I can find all in a row
      Those pretty lines and all?

Large Girl (*seated*)—

  My darling child, the shining sun
   Sends rays on drops of rain,
  To make the bow so finely hung
   Amid the clouds' domain.

  God knoweth all things, sees them all,
   The bow his mandates fill;
  The tiny drops and shining ball
   Reflect His promise still.
       —*Mrs. Emily M. Boyden.*

WHAT A LITTLE BOY IS WORTH.

I'm not worth much in pocket. See! (*turns pockets inside out*). I'm not worth much if you reckon by size. I'm not worth much, folks, so far as wisdom goes. But you wait! I'm growing up to be a man, I am! Mother says I will be one before she is! Besides, she thinks I'm worth something, for I heard her say this morning, that I was worth my weight in gold! *And my Mother knows.*
       —*Practical Teacher.*

NONSENSE ALPHABET.

[*For 26 children. Each has a letter. All speak to A.*]
 All.—

A tumbled down and hurt his Arm against a bit of wood.
 B.—
" My Boy, oh! do not cry; it cannot do you good."
 C.—
" A Cup of Coffee hot can't do you any harm."
 D.—
" A Doctor should be fetched and he would cure the arm."
 E.—
" An Egg beat up with milk would quickly make him well."
 F.—
" A Fish, if broiled, might cure, if only by the smell."

G.—

" Green Gooseberry cool, the best of cures I hold."

H.—

" His Hat should be kept on to keep him from the cold."

I.—

" Some Ice upon his head will make him better soon."

J.—

" Some Jam, if spread on bread, or given in a spoon."

K.—

" A Kangaroo is here—this picture let him see."

L.—

" A Lamp pray keep alight, to make some barley tea."

M.—

" A Mulberry or two might give him satisfaction."

N.—

" Some Nuts, if rolled about, might be a slight attraction."

O.—

" An Owl might make him laugh, if only it would wink."

P.—

" Some Poetry might be read aloud to make him think."

Q.—

" A Quince I recommend—a Quince. or else a Quail."

R.—

" Some Rats might make him move, if fastened by the tail."

S.—

" A Song should now be sung, in hopes to make him laugh."

T.—

" A Turnip might avail, if sliced or cut in half."

U.—

" An Urn with water hot, placed underneath his chin."

V.—

" I'll stand upon a chair and play a Violin."

W.—

" Some Whiskey-Whizzgiggs fetch, some marbles and a ball."

X.—

" Some double XX ale would be the best of all."

Y.—

"Some Yeast mixed up with salt would make a perfect plaster."

Z.—

"Here is a box of Zinc! Get in, my little master!

We'll shut you up! We'll nail you down! We will, my little master!

We think we've all heard quite enough of this, your sad disaster."   —*Practical Teacher.*

THE WINDS.

[A Recitation for Girls.]

First Girl—

Here am I, the chilly North-wind.
From my home 'mid ice and snow.
How I scatter chills and shivers!
In whatever path I go.

Second Girl—

I am called the gentle South-wind.
From my Southland home I bring
Thoughts of soft blue skies and flowers,
Bees that hum and birds that sing.

Third Girl—

Here am I, the merry East-wind.
From my home among the hills,
I am come to make you joyful,
I would banish all your ills.

Fourth Girl—

I am called the gracious West-wind.
Laden with refreshing showers—
I am hailed by all the people,
Ever welcomed by the flowers.

All. Joining hands—

Yes, we are the Winds!
And we blow, blow, blow.
Whispering each a message,
As we go, go, go.

Popular Educator.   —*E. L. Brown.*

IN SCHOOL AGAIN.

[A small girl should speak this. She should hold a slate covered with fig·
ures with her left arm and hand, and a slate pencil in her right hand. She
should speak very slowly as though considering the subject, or puzzled over it.]

I'm sure that two and three make six,
    And six plus three is eight;
I've counted it on my fingers,
    And worked it on my slate.

But our teacher, if you'll believe it,
    She isn't very bright,
She had it wrong herself, and said
    That *my* work wasn't right.

—*St. Nicholas.*

THE INJURED CHILD.

[Mrs. J. is seated when Mrs. S., with a broken doll, comes in, crying; she
immediately rises.]

Mrs. S.—Mrs. Jones, my baby! do, do send for Dr. Penny.
My baby has broken her neck.

Mrs. J.—What! broken her neck! It can't be true! The
poor child! [*wringing her hands*] What shall we do?

Mrs. S. [*frantically*]—Send for the doctor! Send for the
doctor!

Mrs. J. [*going to the door*]—Biddy! Biddy!

Biddy [*appearing*]—What do you wish, mum?

Mrs. J.—Mrs. Smith's baby has broken her neck.

Biddy [*throwing up her hands*]—O, the dear baby! Is
she dead entirely?

Mrs. S.—No, no! Get Dr. Penny.

Biddy [*going out*]—That I will, and quickly too!

Mrs. S. [*together*] —O, my baby will die!
Mrs. J. —O, your baby will die!

    [*Enter Doctor and Biddy.*]

Biddy—Here's the doctor.

Doctor [*laying down hat and coat*]—What's the matter?

Biddy —O, the baby is 'most killed dead!

Mrs. S. [*together*]—My child, O, my child!

Mrs. J. —Mrs. Smith's baby has broken her neck!

Dr. [*crossly*]—Be still! Don't all talk at once.

All—O, O, O!

Dr. [*taking up hat*]—I guess I'll go.

All—No, no, no!

Mrs. S.—My baby's neck is broken!

Dr.—Let me see it [*examines*].   That is a compound fracture.

Mrs. S. [*anxiously*]—Will she die?

Dr.—Not necessarily. Rub this [*gives her a bottle*] on her neck twice a day and keep her warm [*takes up hat and coat*]. Good-day [*goes*].

Ladies [*together*] —Good-day!
Biddy —My blessin' wid ye.

—*Helen W. Boyden.*

WHICH LOVED BEST?

[*Concert Recitation for School.*]

"I love you, mother," said little John;
Then, forgetting his work, his cap went on,
And he was off to the garden swing,
And left her wood and water to bring.

"I love you, mother," said rosy Nell;
"I love you better than tongue can tell."
Then she teased and pouted full half the day,
Till her mother rejoiced when she went to play.

"I love you, mother," said little Fan;
"To-day I'll help you all I can;
How glad I am that school doesn't keep!"
So she rocked the baby till it fell asleep.

Then stepping softly she fetched the broom,
And swept the floor and tidied the room;
Busy and happy all day was she,
Helpful and happy as child could be.

"I love you, mother," again they said—
Three little children going to bed;
How do you think that mother guessed
Which of them really loved her best?

DISAPPOINTED.

[Concert Recitation for School.]

A blackbird swings on a blade of grass,
          Loud whistles he.
He cocks his head as the children pass.
" Shall I stay or fly from this tiny lass?"
          " Chee-wee," quoth he.
Little lass tiptoes up so sly,
          " Hush," whispers she.
Blackbird watches with one bright eye,
But whistles away as though none were by,
          " Chee-wee," sings he.
Down comes a hat with a rush through the air,
          " Hurrah," shouts she;
But when lassie looks no captive is there,
For a very small bird can take very good care
          Of himself—" chee-wee."

Good Cheer.   *—Leigh Prescott.*

THE DANDELIONS.

Upon a showery night and still,
    Without a sound of warning,
A trooper band surprised the hill
    And held it in the morning.
We were not waked by bugle notes,
    No cheer our dreams invaded,
And yet, at dawn, their yellow coats
    On the green slopes paraded.

We careless folk the deed forgot,
    Till one day, idly walking,
We marked upon the self-same spot
    A crowd of veterans talking.
They shook their trembling heads and gray
    With pride and noiseless laughter,
When, well a day! they blew away,
And ne'er were heard of after!

                                 —Helen Gray Cone.

TWO LITTLE OLD LADIES.

Two little old ladies—one grave, one gay—
In the self-same cottage lived day by day.
One could not be happy, " because," she said,
" So many children were hungry for bread;"
And she really had not the heart to smile
When the world was so wicked all the while.

The other old lady smiled all day long,
As she knitted or sewed or crooned a song.
She had not time to be sad, she said,
When hungry children were crying for bread.
So she baked and knitted and gave away
And declared the world grew better each day.

Two little old ladies—one grave, one gay.
Now which do you think chose the wiser way?
St. Nicholas.   *—H. Maud Merrill.*

MISTRESS MOUSE.

Mistress Mouse
Built a house
In Mamma's best bonnet;
All the cats
Were catching rats,
And didn't light upon it.

At last they found it
And around it
Sat watching for the sinner;
When, strange to say,
She got away,
And so they lost their dinner.

GRASSHOPPER GREEN.

Grasshopper Green is a comical chap;
He lives on the best of fare;
Bright little breeches and jacket and cap

These are his summer wear.
Grasshopper Green has a dozen wee boys,
    And, as soon as their legs grow strong,
All of them join in his frolicsome joys,
    Humming his merry song.
It's hopperty, skipperty, high and low,
    Summer's the time for fun.

SOMETHING FUNNY.

Dear me! dear me!
Buzzed a little bee,
I'm always making honey,
No time to play,
But work all day;
Isn't it very funny?
Very, very funny?

O, my!   O, my!
Buzzed a little fly,
I'm always eating honey
And yet I play
All the day;
Isn't it very funny?
Very, very funny?

NAUGHTY PIGS.

Three naughty pigs all in one pen
Drank up the milk left by the men.
Then all three, fast as they could,
Dug their way out to find something good.
One naughty pig ran to a bed;
Soon lay the flowers drooping and dead.
Two naughty pigs dug up some seeds,
And left for the boy not even weeds.
Three naughty pigs safe in the pen,
Never will do such digging again.

GOING TO THE MUSEUM.

[*A Street Scene.*]

*Well dressed boy hurries by, followed by another, who calls
out:*—John! John! where are you going in such a hurry, all
dressed, too, in your Sunday best?

John [*turning around*] —To the museum to see the great
wonders.

Tom.—Do you mean the one that has posters *everywhere?*

John —That's the very one.   They have the famous bram-
ble bush that scratched out the eyes of the man who was so
wondrous wise.

Tom —Aren't you afraid to go near it?

John —Ho, ho!   If it hurt *my* eyes I'd jump into the
other bush and scratch them in again.

Tom —What else do you expect to see?

John —The old woman with the identical broom that she
used to sweep the cobwebs from the sky.

Tom —I thought *she* was dead long ago; she used to live
next door to the old woman in the shoe.

John —She is there, too, with her large family and will
give a reception at which the renowned cat violinist will play
—dear me! I can't tell half.   Come with me and see for
yourself; to-day each visitor will receive a snow-ball roasted
by Simple Simon.

Tom —Is that so?   I'd like to taste one.   [*Takes John's
arm and they walk off together.*]

—*Helen W. Boyden.*

THE MOON.

Dear Mother, how pretty the moon looks to-night,
   She was never so cunning before;
Her two little horns are so sharp and so bright,
   I hope she'll not grow any more.

If I were up there with you and my friends,
   We could rock in it nicely, you see;
We would sit in the middle and hold by both ends,
   Oh, what a bright cradle 't would be!

We would call to the stars to keep out of the way,
 Lest we should rock over their toes,
And there we would sit till the dawn of the day,
 And see where the pretty moon goes.

And there we would rock in the beautiful skies,
 Or through the bright clouds we would roam.
We'd see the sun set, and see the sun rise,
 And on the next rainbow come home.

      —*Mrs. Follen.*

WHAT I KNOW.

It is God that made the flowers,
 And careth for them all,
And for our Heavenly Father's love,
 There is not one too small.

PAPA'S STORY.

A fairy once entered
 The heart of a rose,
And said: " This is lovely!
 And do you suppose
That if I should live here
 Till June days are o'er,
That any intruder
 Would enter my door?"

Just then a big bumble-bee,
 Passing that way,
Came in without knocking,
 Determined to stay.
"Ah, me!" said the fairy,
 " You frighten me so."
And thrust a rose thorn
 Thro' the bumble bee's toe.

      —*Mrs. S. J. Brigham.*

THE DANDELIONS.

Dainty little dandelions
  Smiling on the lawn,
Sleeping thro' the dewy night,
  Waking with the dawn.
Pretty little dandelions,
  Sleeping in the glen,
When another year returns
  They will come again.

JACK FROST'S LITTLE SISTER.

This morning when all the rest had gone down,
  I stood by the window to see
The beautiful pictures which there in the night,
  Jack Frost had been making for me.

There were mountains and mills, and bridges and boats,
  Some queer looking houses and trees,
A hammock that swung by itself in the air,
. And a giant cut off at the knees.

Then there was a steeple so crooked and high,
  I was thinking it surely must fall,
When right down below it I happened to spy
  The loveliest thing of them all.

The cutest and cunningest dear little girl,
  I looked at her hard as I could;
And she stood there so dainty, and looked back at me,
  In a little white ulster and hood.

" Good morning," I whispered, for all in a flash,
  I knew 'twas Jack Frost's little sister;
I was so glad to have her come visiting me,
  I reached up quite softly and kissed her.

There!—can you believe it?—the darling was gone,
  Killed dead in that one little minute!
I never once dreamed that a kiss would do that,
  Nor could there be any harm in it.

But I am so sorry! for though I have looked
　　Fifty times at that window since then.
Half hoping to see her once more, yet I know
　　She never can come back again.

And it may be foolish, but all through the day,
　　I have felt—and I knew that I should—
Just as if I had killed her, that dear baby-girl
　　In a little white ulster and hood.

—*Youth's Companion.*

A SPEECH.

[For a very little Boy.]

The boys all said I was too small
To make a speech before you all.
I know I'm not as large as they,
But I've something I'd like to say.
I don't know how to say it quite
I've only thought a little mite.
'Tis how to thank all these friends here
And wish you'd come again next year.
I have not said it like the rest,
But I have done my very best;
And your attention ere we part,
I thank you for with all my heart.
　　[Place hand on the heart.]

–*L. Crosby.*

TRUTH AND DUTY.

I know one thing—if I stand by the principles of truth and duty, nothing can inflict upon me any permanent harm.

—*Horace Mann.*

SPRING TIME.

First Child—

" Oh, the spring has come," chirped the dear little birds,
　　As they opened their drowsy eyes,
And shook out their fans in their pretty tails,

And turned up their heads to the skies.
"'Tis time now to look for a place to build."
So Robin engaged an elm-tree;
The black Crow, she spoke for a tall pine's top,
Where high in the world she might be.

Second Child—

The Sparrow took lease of an old ox-track,
With grasses to thatch it all o'er.
"I like a low cottage," she said to herself,
"With a daisy to nod by the door."
The Swallow, she fancied the corner lot
Of the barn, 'neath the sloping eaves;
The Oriole sought for a graceful twig,
Where her cradle could rock with the breeze.

First Child—

"The spring has come," said each little flower
As she stirred in her damp brown bed;
First Snowdrop peeped in her neat white cap,
Then modestly hung down her head.
"Do I hear Sir Robin?" said Crocus white,
"I am certainly late," cried she;
Then popped out her head from under the clothes,
And looked straight into the tree.

Third Child—

The Mayflower woke, and she drew from the moss
On which she had pillowed her head,
Her small waxen phials of odorous sweets
To perfume her soft lowly bed.
"'Tis darksome down here," moaned Violet blue;
But when she crept out to the sky,
She had to slip back behind a green leaf,
'Twas so bright for her tender young eye.

Fourth Child—

"These rich golden beams," said Buttercup gay,
"I'll take to my daisy brown,
And churn them and pat them in bright little balls,
The green of my young buds to crown."

"Oh, there is a bee!" cried Miss Clover so red,
　"He's buzzing because I'm not up;"
So she sprang into sight with her sweet honey-jars,
　And asked Mr. Bee in, to sup.

All—

A busy time is this fresh bright spring
　For birdie and bee and for flowers;
There's work for each in its own little world,
　And joy just the same as in ours.

Home and School.　　　　　　　　　　　　—*Mary Gordon.*

GRANDMA'S VISIT.

[*While Mother is tidying the room she looks up and sees an old lady with bonnet, shawl and specs, approaching. She turns to the children, playing with their dolls, and says*]—Here comes dear Grandma; run, Margaret Sophronia and Susan Jane, run and meet her.

Children [*running*]—We are so glad to see you, dear, dear Grandma [*kiss her*]. What did you bring to us?

Grandma—O, you little rogues! I did not forget what you like best. Here are bags of candy and peanuts.

[*Gives the bags to the children, and they run back to their Mother, saying*]—O, mamma, mamma! See what Grandma has brought to us!

Mother—What a good Grandma you have! Now sit down and be very good while she is here. [*Grandma enters slowly.*] I am so glad to see you, Grandma! [*kisses her.*] Why, you haven't been here in an age! I was afraid you were ill.

Grandma—I am getting to be an old woman and tire so easily that I can't come any oftener. But it was such a fine day I thought I would walk over and find out how you and the children were.

Mother—We are quite well. Let me help you take off your things [*removes her things and offers a chair*]. Sit down and rest, dear Grandma, while I get a cup of tea for you.

Grandma [*seating herself*]—Thank you, I will.

Mother [*bringing tea and cake*]—Here is the tea and a bit of cake.

Grandma [*smelling the tea*]—How fragrant the tea is! How do you make it?

Mother—A teaspoonful of tea to a quart of boiling water is my invariable rule.

Grandma—Is not that rather strong? [*sipping the tea.*]

Mother—I think not.

Grandma [*holding out cup*]—A little more water, please.

[*Mother pours in some water and then sits down. Grandma eats the cake and drinks the tea while they talk.*]

Mother—How is dear Grandpa?

Grandma—He is getting to be quite feeble.

Mother—And the rest of the family?

Grandma—They are all well except Jeremiah. He went over to the park to see a baseball game yesterday, when he ought to have been at home bringing in coal. Of course he caught cold.

Mother—Did you have to call in the doctor?

Grandma—O, no! Grandpa applied strong birch at once, and it warmed him right up; but he does not care to go out much at present.

Mother—Birch! Is not that a new medicine?

Grandma—O, no! child! it is an old woman's remedy.

Mother—Would it not be good for Susan Jane and Margaret Sophronia?

Grandma—Excellent, excellent! no better remedy in the world for children.

Mother—I'll write it down. [*writes.*]

Grandma [*rising*]—I feel very much rested and refreshed. I must go now so as to get home before dark.

Mother [*helping to put on shawl and bonnet*]—I am so sorry you can't stay longer, but do come oftener.

Children [*crowding around her*]—Yes, yes, and bring us us more candy and peanuts.

Grandma [*kissing them*]—Good-by, dears.

All—Good-by.

—*Helen W. Boyden.*

*AUTUMN LEAVES.

"Come, little leaves," said the wind one day—
"Come over the meadows with me and play.
Put on your dresses of red and gold;
Summer is gone and the days grow cold."

Soon as the leaves heard the winter's loud call,
Down they came fluttering, one and all;
Over the brown fields they danced and flew,
Singing the soft little songs they knew;

"Cricket, good-bye, we've been friends so long.
Little brook, sing us your farewell song,—
Say you're sorry to see us go;
Ah! you *are* sorry, right well we know.

"Dear little lambs, in your fleecy fold,
Mother will keep you from harm and cold;
Fondly we've watched you in vale and glade;
Say, will you dream of your loving shade?"

Dancing and whirling the little leaves went;
Winter had called them and they were content.
Soon fast asleep in their earthy beds
The snow laid a coverlet over their heads.

THE LITTLE GRANDMA.

[Little girl comes in; sits in a big chair; puts on the cap and glasses lying near, and tries to knit while she talks.]

Now, I will be dear Grandma,
And sit in Grandma's chair;
Put on her cap and glasses,
And smooth away my hair,
And think of things that happened
So many years ago,
And knit my long white stocking
Until I reach the toe.

But if at last my Grandma
Should come inside the door,
And find a nice old lady
She never saw before,
And ask me, quite politely,
To stay with her to tea,
I never could refuse her;
Could *you*, if you were me?

—Mrs. S. J. Brigham.

DOCTOR SPARROW.

One morning as Doctor Sparrow, the wise,
  Was going his patients to see,
He spied a young frog lying stretched on the ground,
  All alone at the foot of a tree.

"What ails you, poor fellow?" he kindly inquired,
  "I'm afraid you must be very ill,
And this place is *so damp!* I'm sure that you need,"
  Said wise Dr. Sparrow, "a pill!

"Your eyes are as heavy as lead, and your hands
  Are terribly cold; so I pray
That you take one of these every hour, and beware
  How you go near the water to-day!"

Now imagine the doctor's dismay, if you can,
  When up sprang the frog from the grass,
Crying out, "I'm obliged, but I really don't think
  That I need your advice.   Let me pass!"

With a croak, and a trill, and a rollicking laugh,
  "Ho, ho! Ha, ha, ha! He, he, he!
I believe in the *water-cure* treatment, dear sir,
  So don't waste your pellets on me!"

MEADOW TALK.

[*Concert Recitation for School.*]

A bumble-bee, yellow and gold,
  Sat perched on a red-clover top,

When a grass-hopper, wiry and old,
   Came along with a skip and a hop.
"Good morrow!" cried he, "Mr. Bumble-bee!
   You seem to have come to a stop."

"We people that work,"
   Said the bee, with a jerk,
"Find a benefit sometimes in stopping;
   Only insects like you,
Who have nothing to do,
   Can keep up a perpetual hopping."

The grass-hopper paused on his way,
   And thoughtfully hunched up his knees:
"Why trouble this sunshiny day,"
   Quoth he, "with reflections like these?
I follow the trade for which I was made:
   We all can't be wise bumble-bees."

"There's a time to be sad,
   And a time to be glad;
A time for both working and stopping;
   For men to make money,
For you to make honey,
   And for me to do nothing but hopping."

———

THE SLING-SHOT.

A robin's song the whole day long
   In an apple-tree was heard,
A thoughtless boy with a deathly toy
   Bent over a dying bird.
The song was hushed, a heart was crushed,
   A widow bird's low moan
Upon the breeze, died in the trees,
   A nest was left alone.
O would that words, sweet baby birds,
   Could soothe her sorrow now!

Nestle and rest in your tiny nest
   In the fragrant apple bough.
Her heart would break but for your sake,
   Yet mother love is strong;
Her little brood must have its food
   Or earth would miss its song.
Sleep, darlings, then she'll come again
   When grief's wild storm is o'er,
Tho' her mate's sweet song that made her strong
   Is hushed forevermore.

—John Kelly.

THE SICK CHILD.

Mamma rises, and places doll in the cradle beside her, saying—There, dear daughter, lie in the cradle awhile and let mamma sew. [*Resumes her seat, and, while sewing, sings a lullaby;* * *at its conclusion doctor knocks and walks in.*]

Doctor—How do you do, Madame; how is the little girl to-day?

Mamma [*putting down work and taking doll*]—Very sick indeed. She wants me to hold her all of the time.

Dr.—Sleep much?

M.—Yes, but with her eyes wide open.

Dr. [*gravely*]—That's a very serious matter. Doesn't she wink?

M.—No, not at all. [*Doctor looks at doll.*]

Dr. [*in a surprised tone*]—Why, she has only *one* eye!

M. [*indignantly*]—Don't I know it?

Dr. [*very crossly*]—You *said* eyes. Cry any?

M.—Only when she is pinched!

Dr. [*wisely, as he slyly pinches doll*]—Very complicated disease.

M.—Stop hurting my sick child, you cruel doctor!

Dr. [*very severely*]—If you wish me to cure her, Madame, you must let me do as I please.

M. [*crying as the doctor pinches her*]—Don't pinch too hard then.

* *Em's Lullaby. Auntie Em's Song Leaves.*

Dr.—I am only testing her lungs. She is threatened with brain fever.

M.—O, no, no, Doctor; that is dreadful [*wailing*]. My poor dear darling! It can't be true!

Dr. [*loftily*]—I know what I am talking about. Cut off her hair and keep her in the house.

M.—O, dear! O, dear! I can't do that!

Dr. [*crossly*]—Why not?

M.—She must sing at the concert on Tuesday evening, for Destitute Heathen; there is Mrs. Smith's party on Wednesday—she must not miss that; on Thursday will come the dancing lessons, and on Friday she will play a piano solo for the Assembled Knights. I can't have her look like a fright at these places! What shall I do? [*thinks*] O, I know. I will keep her home from school this week.

Dr.—You are very sensible. I have no doubt but that her sickness is due to overstudy. Children are crammed now-a-days. Good-day.

—Helen W. Boyden.

THE LITTLE CHIEF.

I'm my mother's little man,
I'm the chief of all the clan.
There's Ned and Fred and Ted,
If you please, sir, *I'm* the Head!

They like their play, and so, you see,
Who's left to be the *man* but *me?*
My mother knows that I am the one
To do the things that *must* be done.

I sweep the walks, I tend the door,
I go her errands to the store—
O, *any* day I'd go a mile
To see my pretty mother smile!

You needn't laugh because I'm small!
Just being big, sir, isn't all—
I'm as *much* a man as *any* man
If I do everything I can!

SPEECH FOR A LITTLE BOY.

Say, boys, I want to tell you something. I want to know if you wouldn't think it very queer if you should go home feeling awfully blue, and looking as long faced as a judge, and your mamma should laugh at you? Well, that's what happened to me to-day. I said, " Mamma, won't you please mend my pocket, 'cause when I put things into it they go way down through ? " She put her thimble right on, so I thought I wouldn't mind if she did smile a little. But before she began to mend she said, "I think, Freddie, that we'd better take the things out below the pocket before we begin to sew it." What *do* you think we found? I had lost so *many* things lately, and there they all were. My top and ball, and the knife that I made such a fuss about, and my mittens, and a handkerchief, and some pennies that I thought somebody *must* have stolen. I 'spose if I'd been a girl I'd have cried my eyes out, but *I* didn't cry. I just waited, and when mamma found all those things, I just laughed too. I *thought* that coat was pretty heavy.

AUTUMN FASHIONS.

The Maple owned that she was tired of always wearing green,
She knew that she had grown, of late, too shabby to be seen!

The Oak and Beech and Chestnut then deplored their shab-
    biness,
And all, except the Hemlock sad, were wild to change their
    dress.

" For fashion-plate we'll take the flowers," the rustling Maple
    said,
"And like the Tulip I'll be clothed in splendid gold and
    red! "

" The cheerful Sunflower suits me best," the lightsome Beech
    replied;
" The Marigold my choice shall be "—the Chestnut spoke with
    pride.

The sturdy Oak took time to think—"I hate such glaring
    hues;
The Gillyflower, so dark and rich, I for my model choose."

So every tree in all the grove, except the Hemlock sad,
According to its wish, ere long in brilliant dress was clad.

And here they stand through all the soft and bright October
    days;
They wish to be like flowers—indeed, they look like huge
    bouquets!
Wide Awake.   —*Edith M. Thomas.*

WHAT I WANT.

I want a piece of calico
    To make my doll a dress.
I don't want a big piece;
    A yard'll do, I guess.

I wish you'd fred my needle,
    And find my fimble too;
I has such heaps o' sewin',
    I don't know what to do.

My Hepsy tore her apron
    A-tum'lin' down the stair;
And Cæsar's lost his pantaloons,
    And needs anozzer pair.

I want my Maud a bonnet,—
    She hasn't none at all;
And Fred must have a jacket,—
    His ozzer one's too small.

I want's to go to grandma's,
    You promised me I might;
I know she'd like to see me,
    I wants to go to-night.

She lets me wash the dishes,
  And see in grandpa's watch,
I wish I d free four pennies,
  To buy some butter-scotch.

I wants some newer mittens,—
  I wish you'd knit me some;
'Cause most my finger freezes,
  They leak so in the fum.

I wored 'em out last winter
  A-pullin' Georgie's sled.
I wish you wouldn't laugh so,
  It hurts me in my head.

I wish I had a cooky,
  I'm hungry as I can be;
If you hasn't pretty large ones,
  You'd better bring me free.

LATE.

The minute hand points to the quarter
  And Jennie is there at the gate;
The clock is too fast, I am certain—
  It always is fast when I'm late.
There! Jennie has gone on without me;
  Mean thing! pray, why couldn't she wait?

Has any one seen my examples?
  Please, mother, help look for my slate,
I wonder who has had the shoe-hook?
  My pencil has dropped in the grate.
How everything hinders a person,
  So sure as a person is late.
                    —*Harper's Young People.*

CHARLEY'S TRUMPET.

I've got Charley's trumpet;
  Every body knows it;

[*Blows a trumpet.*]
It makes a *great* sensation
Every time I blow it!

[*Blows trumpet.*]
If you've got the *headache*
Don't come *too* near it.

[*Blows trumpet*]
Won't you stop and listen
Just for half a minute?
Only let me show you
About how much noise there is in it.
[*Blows vigorously as he leaves the platform.*]

A NEW MOTHER HUBBARD.

Miss Polly Betsey Patterson
In a Mother Hubbard cloak
And a Mother Hubbard bonnet,
With a most bewitching poke,

One morning met a curly dog,
He was of medium size—
His ears were drooped, his tail was limp,
And the tears stood in his eyes.

Said Polly to the curly dog:
" Why do you look so sad?"
" Because," replied he, with a sniff,
" The times are very bad.

"You see," said he, "the streets are full
Of little Mother Hubbards,
But though I've wagged my tail 'most off,
They never speak of cupboards."

Said Polly Betsey: " Come with me,
'T would melt a heart of stone!
I'll give you lots of bread and milk,
And a juicy mutton-bone."

She took him home and fed him well;
His tears were turned to laughter;
And now, wherever Polly goes,
The curly dog trots after.

—*St Nicholas.*

MOTHER'S TRIALS.

[Two girls, both wearing long dresses. Mrs. J. knocks; Mrs. C. sewing, rises.]

Mrs. C.—Dear me! There is some one at the door. I wonder how I look [*looks in glass and arranges hair. Mrs. J. knocks again*]. I wish people would not call so early [*goes to door*].

Mrs. J.—How do you do? I have come to visit with you a little while this afternoon.

Mrs. C.—I am so glad to hear you say so. Step right in and take off your things [*removes bonnet*]. Pray, be seated. How are the children?

Mrs. J.—They are all well, excepting the twins and John and James and Fan and Tom; they have the measles.

Mrs. C. [*taking up her work*]—I hope you will excuse my sewing, but I have not made the children's summer dresses yet, and warm weather will soon be here.

Mrs. J. [*sighing*]—I don't know when I'll do mine! My cook left yesterday, and I have everything to do myself.

Mrs. C.—She was such a good girl too. *I* never have *any* trouble with *my* girls. Why did she leave?

Mrs. J.—Just because the twins and John and Jane and Fan and Tom and the rest of the children—poor dears—wanted to eat between meals. Suppose they do get a few crumbs around, I buy the food and she ought to be thankful that I don't make her pay for the wasted crumbs.

Mrs. C.—Cooks *are* such a trial! Mothers have hard times! [*Mrs. J. rises and puts on her bonnet.*] Don't put on your things, stay to tea.

Mrs. J.—Don't ask me to stay. I must hurry, for I expect the children will get into mischief while I am away. Come to see me.

Mrs. C.—O, certainly! I'll come to-morrow and stay all day. [*Enter cook.*]

Cook—Sure, mum, I am after tellin' ye that I am goin' to leave.

Mrs. C.—What, going to leave? [*Mrs. J. smiles.*]

Cook—Well, yes. I can't be workin' so hard. I must have Saturday and Sunday and Wednesday to myself *every* week, and some weeks I need two more days off.

Mrs. J. [*smiling*]—I thought *you* never had *any* trouble with your girls. Good-by.

Mrs. C.—O, you horrid thing! [*Exit, crying.*]

—*Helen W. Boyden.*

TELL-TALE OF SPRING.

[*Concert Recitation for School.*]

I've found out Spring's secret;
I know why she's late;
The mischief, the truant,
She cares not who wait,
Who freeze and who shiver
And pine for the sight
Of one yellow daffy
Or violet white.
Ah, yes; I've her secret;
I'll give and not sell;
I'll tell it, I'll tell it,
My tongue burns to tell—
The mischief, the truant,
No wonder she's late,
Coming all the way round
By the Golden Gate!
Yes, that's where I tracked her;
I caught her to-day
Lying down by a river
With lambkins at play,
The mischief, the vagrant,
The spendthrift, I swear
She was tossing roses

Aloft in the air;
As children toss bubbles,
To shine one by one,
And float for a minute
Then die in the sun.
Her grass lay all scattered,
Who chose, helped themselves;
The hills were like velvet
Spread green for the elves.

H. H.

THE RIVULET.

Run, little rivulet, run!
Summer is fairly begun.
Bear to the meadow the hymn of the pines,
And the echo that rings where the waterfall shines.
Run, little rivulet, run!

Run, little rivulet, run!
Sing to the fields of the sun,
That wavers in emerald, shimmers in gold,
Where you glide from your rocky ravine, crystal-cold
Run, little rivulet, run!

Run, little rivulet, run!
Stay not till summer's done!
Carry the city the mountain bird's glee;
Carry the joys of the hills to the sea;
Run, little rivulet, run!

—Lucy Larcom.

WHAT I MUST REMEMBER.

It is easier not to speak a word at all than not speak more
words than we should. *—Thos. à Kempis.*

DOLLY'S PUNISHMENT.
[Girl with doll.]

Go right in the closet, my dolly girl,
I'm sorry you've been so bad;

But your conduct is dreadful and makes my hair
   'Most gray, and my poor heart sad.

Go and reflect how wicked you are,
   And not in the least like your little mamma,
I hope, that in the future, you really will try
   To be just as obedient a daughter as I.

CHERRY-TIME.

[Little girl with cherries.]

Cherry-time is it? and what do we see
But little Miss Alice who's been to the tree
And gathered as many as pockets will hold.
And now lest my Auntie and Grandma may scold,
I have brought a peace offering of cherries you know,
A handful that into my pockets won't go.
A liberal proceeding, you think? but, dear me!
I will throw in the bargain—sweet kisses, you see.

A THOUGHT.

Education is not confined to books,
   The world is a great school.
                    —*J. T. Trowbridge.*

MY MEDICINE BOTTLE.

Yes, this is my medicine bottle,   (*holds it up.*)
Mamma sent me up stairs to find.
It's all very well for my mother,
But *I* think it's really unkind
To make *me* take stuff that is bitter,
And horrid to swallow, dear me!
If I were a little girl's mother
What a different mother I'd be.
My child should have nothing but sugar,
And candy and things that are sweet;
And I *never* would tell her she couldn't
Have just all she wanted to eat.

RECITATION FOR CLASS.

First Pupil—

 We are busy little bees,
  We are workers one and all;
 We try our teacher dear to please,
  We're bright, although we're small.

Second Pupil—

 We must come to school each day,
  If we would wiser grow;
 In the pleasant month of May,
  And through the winter's snow.

Third Pupil—

 Day by day and year by year,
  We'll climb the ladder high;
 We'll never fail, we need not fear,
  With the motto " We will try."

Fourth Pupil—

 The great wide world before us lies,
  There's work for us to do;
 If we would win the victor's prize,
  We must be brave and true.

      —*Sylvia Manning.*

THE FIGURES.

[Eleven pupils, with large figures, stand in a half circle exposing the figures that they hold while they speak.]

 1. This is figure one,
   Now that task is done.

 2. This is figure two,
   As well as we can do.

 3. This is figure three;
   As crooked as it can be.

 4. This is figure four;
   Would you like to see some more?

5. This is figure five;
    It looks almost alive.

6. This is figure six,
    Wait and see its tricks.

7. This is figure seven;
    Luck to it is given.

8. This is figure eight;
    You can never get it straight.

9. This is figure nine;
    Last of all the line.

0. Wait, another we have got!
    This is cipher, counts for naught.

10. Placed upon the right, and then
    One and cipher gives us ten.

20. So they go, and there are plenty,
    Till they reach the number twenty.

SAM'S WHITEWASHING.

'Pears strange to me, it do indeed,
Why Chloe so black should be;
Now all the other babies around,
Are white, exceptin' she.
I rolled her once in flour, I did,
But the flour wouldn't stick;
She yelled and screamed so awful loud,
I washed her mighty quick.
I'll bet dere mus' be sumfin'
That makes the white folks white;
It mus' be whitewash—so it mus'.
Now, baby Chloe, keep quiet,
I'll get the whitewash out de shed,
Dad mixed it up dis morn;
Just you lie still, I'll make you white,

As shuah as you is born.
O laws! what makes you go and yell?
Keep on, and mammy'll hear,
And if she does, she won't take long
To lif' me by the ear.
Now, Chloe, just stop your screechin',
You ain't got any sense,
A'cryin' so, and you as white
As ole Joe Pearson's fence.
I tole yer mammy'd hear yer,
She's comin' mighty spry,—
I hates to leab' de job half done,
But 'pears I'd better fly.

School and Home.   *—M. Nolan.*

WELCOME.

[Have seven girls, with large letters, stand in a row, exposing the letters
they hold when they speak.]

All—

O, swiftly the long weeks have slipped away;
Now study time's over, we're ready for play,
But, ere we begin we've come here to meet you,
And seven wee lasses we greet you.

First Girl—

I come the first, and full in view
I hold up *my* letter, this big W.

Second Girl—

I am second, and all can see
The one *I* hold is the letter E.

Third Girl—

So straight and tall, you all can tell
The one I hold is the letter L.

Fourth Girl—

If you look at me you'll all agree,
The one *I* have is the letter C.

Fifth Girl—

> So big and round, you surely know
> The one I bear is the letter O.

Sixth Girl—

> Five letters you've seen, and after them
> I hold up mine, 'tis the letter M.

Seventh Girl—

> The very last I must surely be.
> Would you know my name? I'm the letter E.

All—

> And now, if you'd know the story we tell,
> A glad word of greeting gladly we spell,
> We are W–e–l–c–o–m–e.

Popular Educator.   —*Bertha Aubert.*

A BIRTHDAY GIFT.

[Little girl, with apron full of apples.]

> The latch is so high
>   On this great big door,
> And I've so many apples
>   In my pinafore!
> I got them for Mamma—
>   This is her birthday—
> And I know when she sees them
>   Just what she will say
> O, what shall I do?
>   Hark! a step in the hall!
> Hurry, O, hurry!
>   My apples will fall!
>   [*Runs into dressing room.*]

SUMMER TIME.

> To hear the light winds play around
> From leaf to leaf with rustling sound—
> And trill of birds and insects hum,
> And all the lulling tones that come
>   In summer time.   —*W. W. Caldwell.*

A BOUQUET.

[Four girls, with appropriate flowers.]

Dandelion—

> I am the dandelion,
>   Yellow as you see;
> And when the children see me
>   They shout for glee.
> I grow by every wayside,
>   And when I've had my day
> I spread my wings so silvery [*spreads arms*]
>   And fly away.

Forget-me-not—

> When God made all the flowers
>   He gave each one a name,
> And when all the others had gone,
>   A little blue one came,
> And said, in trembling whisper,
>   "My name has been forgot,"
> Then the good Father called her,
>   "Forget-me-not."

Fern—

> A fern the people call me,
>   I'm always clothed in green,
> I live in every forest;
>   You've seen me oft. I ween.
> Sometimes I leave the shadow
>   To grow beside the way,
> You'll see me as you pass.
>   Some nice fine day.

Violet—

> I am the little violet;
>   In my purple dress,
> I hide myself so safely,
>   That you'd never guess
> There was a flower so near you,
>   Nestling at your feet.
> And that's why I send you
>   My fragrance sweet.

[A pretty effect is secured by having the girls' dresses white and trimmed with appropriate colors.]

SPRING AND THE GARDEN.

When Spring went into the garden,
    Her holiday time to keep,
She walked about in the dawning
    And found the flowers all asleep.

So first she wakened the snowdrops,
    And washed their faces with rain,
And then she fed them with sunlight,
    And gave them white frocks again.

The crocuses next she summoned,
    In purple stripes and yellow,
And she bade the south wind shake them
    Till each one kissed his fellow.

The nodding daffodils heard her,
    And courtesied low as he passed,
Each blossom dropped like a pennon
    Hung out from a tall green mast.

Into the violets' eyes she looked,
    And spoke till she made them hear,
" What are you dreaming now? " she asked.
    They answered, " That Spring is here! "

And then the trees stretched their fingers,
    And opened their curled up leaves,
And the birds who sat and watched them
    Flew straight to their cool, green eaves.

One made her nest in the ivy,
    And one in the apple-tree;
But the thrush showed hers in secret
    To the south wind and the bee!

— M. Henderson.

SEWING.

[Little girl, sewing, looks up and appears to be talking to her doll, sitting near.]

    No, I am quite too busy
      To go out doors and play,

This hemming will keep me working
  As hard as I can all day.
Sometimes I forget which finger
  Goes under the little hem,
Or which one should have the thimble,
  It fits either one of them.

Sometimes my thread gets tangled
  Or slips from the little eye;
Sometimes I prick my finger
  Till I—well—almost cry.
But there do you see the stitches
  All in a little row?   [*holds up the sewing.*]
My darling dolly's handkerchief
  Is finished, and she can go.
                                 —*Sidney Dayre.*

THE DIAMONDS.

[*Concert Recitation for School.*]

A million little diamonds
  Twinkled on the trees,

[*Raise hands and move fingers.*]

And all the little maidens said,
  " A jewel if you please! "

[*Outstretch hands.*]

But while they held their hands outstretched,
  To catch the diamonds gay.
A million little sunbeams came,
  And stole them all away.

[*Fold arms gently.*]

A QUEER COUPLE.

Once a hopper and a spider
  Promenaded down the street.
Said the hopper to the spider:
  " Smile to all we chance to meet."

Said the spider to the hopper,
   Slyly glancing at her spouse:
"Do you really think it proper
   Thus to recognize a mouse?"

Then her spouse began to chide her
   For her foolish pride of life;
"Don't you know you're but a spider,
   Notwithstanding you're my wife?"

But the hopper vainly plied her
   With his questions quick and keen.
She replied, "Altho' a spider,
   I'm as good as you, I ween."

Thus the spider and the hopper
   Promenading down the street,
In deciding what was proper
   All their friends forgot to greet.

—*William B. Oleson.*

KINDNESS.

Kind hearts are the gardens,
Kind thoughts are the roots,
Kind words are the blossoms,
Kind deeds are the fruits.

SOW, SEW, SO.

Boy (sowing)—

   So the farmers sow!
   Busy, busy, all the day,
While the children are at play,
Stowing, stowing, close away
Baby wheat and rye in bed,
So the children may be fed.
   So, so, so.

Girl (sewing)—

   Sew, sew, sew,
   So the mothers sew,
  Busy, busy, all the day,
  While the children are at play,
  Sewing, sewing fast away
  So the children may have frocks,
  Trousers, coats, and pretty socks.
    So, so, so.

Both (sowing and sewing)—

   Sow, sew, so.
   So they sow and sew.

Boy—

  S and O and W,
  This is what the farmers do;

Girl—

  Put an E in place of O,
  This is how the mothers sew,

Both—

  So they sow and sew for you,
   So without the W,
   So, so, so.   —*Rose Graham.*

A MISTAKE.

The man in the moon who sails in the skies
 Is a most courageous skipper;
  But he made a mistake
   When he tried to take
 A drink of milk from the dipper.
He dipped it into the milky way,
 And slowly cautiously filled it,
  But the little bear growled,
  And the great bear howled,
 And frightened him so he spilled it.
     —*St. Nicholas.*

A MISTAKE.

A Tadpole sat on a cold, gray stone,
  And sadly thought of his life,
" Alas, must I live all alone," said he,
  " Or shall I espouse me a wife? "

A wise old Frog, on the brink of the stream,
  Leaned over, and said, with a sigh:
" O, wait till you're older, my dear young friend
  You'll have better taste by-and-by!

" Girls change, you know, and the Pollywog slim,
  That takes your fancy to-day,
May not be the Polly at all you'd choose
  When the summer had passed away."

But the Tadpole rash thought he better knew,
  And married a Pollywog fair.
And before the summer was over, he sat
  On the brink of that stream in despair.

For, would you believe it? his fair young bride
  Proved to be but a stupid frog,
With never a trace of the beauty and grace
  Of young Miss Pollywog.

And although the Tadpole himself had grown
  Stout and stupid, too,
He only saw the faults of his wife
  (As others sometimes do).

To all young Tadpoles my moral is this:
  Before you settle in life,
Be sure you know, without any doubt
  What you want in the way of a wife.

IF.

If all the seas were one sea,
  What a great sea that would be!
And if all the trees were one tree,

What a great tree that would be!
And if all the axes were one ax,
    What a great ax that would be!
And if all the men were one man,
    What a great man that would be!
And if the great man took the great ax,
    And cut down the great tree,
    And let it fall into the great sea,
What a great *splash* that would be!

THE FIRST TIME.

I never spoke before to-day,
    The smallest boy am I,
As I have not much to say,
    I'll only say Good-by.

WHAT I THINK.

I stand before you just so high,
    [raises hand over head]
    A very little girl.
I see so many folks,
    My head is all a-whirl.
I'm frightened 'most, and think that play
    Is better far than this.
And so I'll make a pretty bow,
    [bows]
    And throw you all a kiss.
    [kisses her hand]

A SMART BOY.

[Boy with slate.]

I'm glad I have a good-sized slate
With lots of room to calculate.
Bring on your sums, I'm ready now,
My slate is clean and I know how.

But don't you ask me to *subtract,*
I like to have my slate well packed,
And only two long rows, you know,
Make such a *miserable* show!
And, please, don't bring me sums to *add;*
Well, multiplying's just as bad;
And say, I'd rather not divide;
Bring me something I haven't tried!

-- ------- -

HOW SOAP WAS MADE.

Some water and oil
One day had a broil,
As down in a glass they were dropping;
They could not unite,
But continued to fight,
Without any prospect of stopping.
Some pearlash o'erheard,
And as quick as a word
Jumped into the midst of the clashing;
When all three agreed,
And united with speed,
And soap was created for washing.

TOM'S EYES AND MINE.

My brother Tom is just too mean,
And says the very worst things
About my lovely doll Irene,
Who's just an angel, all but wings.

He says her face is made of wax,
And that her curls are not true hair,
But only common yellow flax,
And that 'tis paint that makes her fair.

Tom's eyes are not like mine, I know;
 Or he could see her almost cry,
To hear him talk about her so,
 And not be able to reply.

But boys are *only* boys, you know,
 You can't expect too much of them,
I only wonder that they grow
 In one and twenty years to men.

Popular Educator. —*L. K. C.*

OUR DUTY.

I think it's not an easy task
 To speak a piece in school,
But still I do not like to ask
 To be excused the rule.

For little boys must some day take
 The places of the men,
And if they would good speakers make,
 Must try and try again.

This be our motto; and now here
 I'll close my little rhyme,
Hoping, should I again appear,
 To better do next time.

—*Good Times.*

OUR BOY'S SPEECH.

I'm not much more than six years old,
 I have not learned to spell,
But yet at school I'm often told,
 I'm doing very well.

My teacher must think me quite wise,
 And easy too, to teach,
Else why should scholars of my size
 Be called on for a speech?

I first must learn to spell and read,
    To make a good oration;
Another thing I know I need,
    A good two months' vacation.
                  —Jas. D. Sturges.

THE BROOK'S SONG.

King Frost comes and locks me up,
    The sunshine sets me free;
I frolic with the grave old trees,
    And sing right cheerily.

I go to see the lady flowers,
    And make their diamond spray;
The birds fly down to chat with me,
    The children come to play.

I am the blue sky's looking glass,
    I hold the rainbow bars;
The moon comes down to visit me,
    And brings the little stars.

Oh, merry, merry is my life,
    As a gypsy's out of Spain!
Till grim King Frost comes from the North,
    And locks me up again.
                  —Mrs. M. F. Butts

THE COMING BLOOM.
First Child—
    When beechen buds begin to swell
    And woods the blue-bird's warble know,
    The yellow violet's modest bell
    Peeps from the last year's leaves below.
                  —Bryant.
Second Child—
    Fair daffodils, we weep to see
      You haste away so soon,
    As yet the early rising sun
      Has not attained its noon.   *—Herrick.*

Third Child—

  The rose in her dark bower lingers,
   But her curtains will soon unclose;
  The lilacs will shake her ringlets
   Over the blush of the rose.

         —Rob't Buchanan.

Fourth Child—

    THE SONG OF THE THISTLE.

  Within my deep and purple flowers,
   In safety rests the wandering bee:
  None else, 'midst odorous summer bowers,
   Regardeth me.

        —Dinah Mulock Craik.

Fifth Child—

  There is a flower, a little flower,
   With silver crest and golden eye,
  That welcomes every changing hour
   And weathers every sky.

  On waste and woodland, rock and plain,
   Its humble buds unheeded rise:
  The rose has but a summer's reign,
   The daisy never dies.

        —Jas. Montgomery.

WHAT WE BELIEVE.

First Boy—

    Each day and every day,
    Do what is right.

         —Cary.

Second Boy—

    Each day and every day,
    Speak the truth.

         —Cary.

Third Boy—

    Every day is the best day in the year.

         —Emerson.

BIRDS AT SCHOOL.

Soon as the weather gits kinder cool,
Den Mister Black Bird starts ter school;
He fly so high in de g'ogorphi,
He larn how all de countries lie.

Jay Bird study in de summer season,
He got sense an' he got reason,
He larns his cunnin' ways right well,
He kin read an' he kin spell.

Ole Mister Crow's de country preacher,
Sunday preach an' Monday teacher;
Foot er de class sets Mister Kildee,
Singin' out A! B! C! D! A! B!

Mister Owl done miss his spellin'.
He's kept in, I hear folks tellin';
Kept in all day, long of books, sah,
Comes out nights wid blinkin' looks, sah.

Robin's head er de class in readin',
All do well, but he's a leadin';
Bes' in 'rithmetic 's de joree,
Hear him count, one, two, three, fo', three.

Ev'ry bird's in de singin' class, oh!
Dee larnin' swif' an' dee larnin' fas', oh!
Chack-a-lack-a-chack-a-lack-lack-lee!
Cha-cha-chee-chee-cha-cha-chee!
                    —*New Orleans Times-Democrat.*

SUMMER VACATION.

I am so happy, so happy all over,
    The secret I'll tell you!
I told it the daisies, the grasses, the clover;
    They promised to keep it all true:
Vacation is coming, will be here right soon;
    No lessons to learn the whole day.

I think it so nice, from the middle of June
  'Till autumn, for frolic and play!
We'll live with the butterflies, blossoms and bees,
  We'll gather the berries so sweet;
Grow brown as the gypsies, in sunshine and breeze,
  And fleet as the deer with our feet!
Good-bye now, kind teacher, and school-mates all dear,
  And, school-house, a good-bye to you,
When vacation is over, we'll come with a cheer,
  The school-life to gladly renew!
                              —*Mrs H. E. Kimball.*

SUPPOSING.

Supposing the grass should forget to grow,
And the wayside rose should forget to blow,
  Because they were tired and lazy;
Supposing children forgot to be kind,
Forgot their lessons, forgot to mind—
  Wouldn't the world seem crazy?

Supposing that strawberries ripened on trees,
And robins and thrushes swam in the seas,
  While mackerel flew in the air;
Supposing the stars in the meadows grew,
And the sky was green and the leaves were blue—
  What a topsey-turvey affair!

Harper's Young People.   —*Mary N. Prescott.*

AN IGNORANT DOLL.

I want to teach my dolly—
  Her ig'rance is obsurd,
I really hate to 'fess it,
  But she cannot spell a word.

Tho' I give her short ezample
  She never gets them done,
For she doesn't know her tables
  As far as one times one.

She pays the best of 'tention,
    And p'r'aps I am too strick,
. But sakes! she tries my patience
    When she studies 'rifm'tic.

She's careless 'bout her writin',
    She scratches like a hen,
And now she's sprained her thumb so bad,
    She can not hold a pen.

She ought to have a lib'ary,
    But what would be the use
To get her books of poickry
    When she can't read Mother Goose?

She must have a ed-ju-ca-tion,
    For her mamma'd die of shame
If dolly should be lost some day
    When she couldn't spell her name.
Youth's Companion.   *—Anna M. Pratt*

"WE RUNNED AWAY."

Two little rascally darlings they stood,
    Hand clasped in hand, and eyes full of glee,
Stock-still in the midst of the crowded street,
    Naughty as ever children could be.

Horses to right of them, horses to left,
    Men hurrying breathless to and fro,
Nobody stopping to wonder at them,
    Nobody there with a right to know.

Oh, what a chance for a full truant joy!
    Earth holds no other equal delight,
Hark! it is over—a shriek fills the air,
    A woman's face flashes pallid white:

"O babies! whose are you? How came you here?"
    The busy street halts aghast, at bay.
Serene smile the infants, as heavenly clear
    They both speak together: "We runned away!"

The crowd and the bustle swayed on again,
　The babies were safe and had lost their fun;
And we who saw, felt a secret pain,
　Half envy of what the babies had done;

And said in our hearts, " Alack! if we tell
　The truth, the whole truth, we must say,
We never get now so good a time
　As we used to have when 'we runned away.' "
Wide Awake.　　　　　　　　　　　　　　—*H. H.*

PUSSY-CLOVER.

[Child has large bunch of pussy-clover.]

Pussy-Clover's running wild,
　Here and there and anywhere,
Like a little vagrant child,
　Free of everybody's care.

Lady-Rose is shy and proud;
　Maiden-Lily bashful-sweet;
Pussy-Clover loves a crowd—
　Seeks the paths of hurrying feet.

Like all faithful, homely things,
　Pussy-Clover lingers on
Till the bird no longer sings,
　And the butterfly is gone.

When the latest asters go,
　When the golden-rod drops dead,
Then, at last, in heaps of snow,
　Pussy-Clover hides her head.

A TRUTH WORTH KNOWING.

For we all have our proper sphere below,
　And this is a truth worth knowing:
You will come to grief, if you try to go
　Where you were never made for going.
　　　　　　　　　　　　—*Phœbe Cary.*

LITTLE FROGS AT SCHOOL.

Twenty froggies went to school
Down beside a rushy pool;
Twenty little coats of green,
Twenty vests all white and clean.
" We must be in time," said they,
" First we study, then we play,
That is how we keep the rule
When we froggies go to school."

Master Bullfrog, brave and stern,
Taught the classes in their turn;
Taught them how to nobly strive,
Likewise how to leap and dive.
From his seat upon the log,
Showed them how to say, " Ker-chog!"
Also how to dodge a blow
From the sticks which bad boys throw.

Twenty froggies grew up fast;
Bullfrogs they became at last;
Not one dunce among the lot,
Not one lesson they forgot.
Polished in a high degree,
As each froggie ought to be,
Now they sit on other logs,
Teaching other little frogs.

DOLLY'S BROKEN ARM.

Mamma, do send for Doctor Man,
  And tell him to be spry;
My dolly fell and broke her arm;
  I'm so afraid she'll die.

I thought that she was fast asleep,
  And laid her on her bed;
But down she dropped upon the floor,
  Oh, dear! she's almost dead!

Poor dolly! she was just as brave,
  And did not cry at all.
Do you suppose she ever can
  Get over such a fall?

But when the doctor mends her arm
  And wraps it up so tight,
Then I will be her little nurse,
  And watch with her all night.

And if she only will get well,
  And does not lose her arm,
I'll never let her fall again,
  Nor suffer any harm.   —*H. L. Charles.*

DANDELIONS.

" I think," said Mother Golden Head,
  To all her children dear,
" I think we'd better be astir,
  And see how things appear."

Then forth she led them one by one,
  Through fields and meadows sweet;
A gayer troop of Golden Heads
  'T is rare for one to meet.

" Good morning, Mistress Golden Head,"
  Said modest Daisy White;
" It seems to me I never saw
  You look so fresh and bright."

" Pray tell me where you've been to find
  Such lovely shining hair;
There's nothing in these parts, I know,
  That can at all compare."

" I think I've only been asleep,
  Yes, fast asleep," she said;
" And while I slept, the fairies poured
  Gold-dust upon my head."   —*Elizabeth A. Davis.*

THE BROWN THRUSH.

There's a merry brown thrush sitting up in a tree,
He's singing to me, he's singing to me!
And what does he say, little girl, little boy?
"Oh, the world's running over with joy!
Don't you hear? don't you see? Hush! look in my tree!
I'm as happy as happy can be."

And the brown thrush keeps singing, " A nest do you see?
And eggs, one, two, three, in the juniper tree?
Don't meddle, don't touch, little girl, little boy,
Or the world will lose some of its joy!
Now I'm glad! now I'm free!
And I always shall be,
If you never bring sorrow to me."

So the merry brown thrush sings away in the tree,
To you and to me, to you and to me;
And he sings all the day, little girl, little boy,
"Oh, the world's running over with joy!
Don't you know, don't you see?
But long it won't be,
Unless we are good as can be."   —*Lucy Larcom.*

HER THIMBLE.

She hunted in the closet,
  She hunted on the stair,
She hunted 'round the door step,
  She hunted everywhere.

She hunted thro' the twilight,
  But, when the dark had come,
She paused to wipe her tears away
  And found it on her thumb!

VACATION.

Good-bye, good-bye to study,
  Vacation now has come,

Vacation now has come;
The days grow hot and sultry,
    The drowsy insects hum.
Our study season's over,
    We've gathered what we could,
We're longing for the meadows now,
    The cool and shady wood.
O, put away the pencils,
    Pile up the slates and books,
We'll go to school with the fishes,
    In their school-rooms in the brooks.

Good-bye, good-bye to teachers,
    Just for a little while,
    Just for a little while;
When summer days are over
    We'll greet you with a smile;

We thank you for your kindness,
    Assistance, care and cheer,
We'll try to please you better in
    Our work another year.
Good-bye, good-bye to schoolmates,
    Vacation fast will fly,
Be merry till it's over.
    And now, good-bye, good-bye.

REMINDING THE HEN.

" It's well I ran into the garden,"
    Said Eddie, his face all aglow,
" For what do you think, mamma, happened?
    You never will guess it, I know.

" The little brown hen was there clucking;
    ' Cut-cut,' she'd say, quick as a wink,
Then ' Cut-cut,' again, only slower,
    And then she would stop short and think.

"And then she would say it all over;
She *did* look so mad an so vext;
For, mamma, do you know, she'd forgotten
The word that she ought to cluck next.

"So *I* said, 'Ca-*daw*-cut,' 'caw-*daw*-cut,'
As loud and as strong as I could,
And she looked 'round at me very thankful;
I tell you, it made her feel good.

"Then she flapped and said, 'Cut-cut-ca-*daw*-cut;'
She remembered just how it went then,
But it's well I ran into the garden—
She might never have clucked right again!"

Christian at Work.   —*Bessie Chandler.*

THE TWO RAINDROPS.

Said a drop to a drop, "Just look at me!
I'm the finest raindrop you ever did see;
I have lived ten seconds, at least, on my pane,
Swelling and filling and swelling again.

"All the little raindrops unto me run,
I watch them and catch them and suck them up, each one;
All the pretty children stand and at me stare,
Pointing with their fingers, 'That's the biggest drop, there.'"

"Yet you are but a drop," the small drop replied;
I don't, myself, see much cause for pride;
The bigger you swell up, we know well, my friend,
The faster you run down, the sooner you'll end."

"Sir," cried the first drop, "Your talk is but dull,
I can't wait to listen for I'm almost full;
You'll run a race with me? No? Then 'tis plain,
I am the largest drop on the whole pane."

Off ran the big drop, at first rather slow;
Then faster and faster, as drops will you know;
Raced down the window-pane, like hundreds before,
Just reached the window-sill—one splash and was o'er.

     —*Dinah M. Craik.*

IN THE STORE.

[Sign over-head, " Bargains To-day." Merchant with goods spread on table before him.]

Gentleman [*coming in*]—How cheap are your best hand-kerchiefs?

M. [*displaying some*]—Only five cents.

G. [*examining*]—That's too much. They aren't worth it.

M.—O, yes; pure linen, fine hem stitched borders.

G.—You'll take two and a half cents, won't you?

M.—No, no; fine goods; they are worth six cents.

G.—I'll give you three cents.

M.—They cost more than that at wholesale.

G. [*throwing the handkerchiefs aside*]—I won't give any more. I can get them cheaper at Smith's. [*Exit.*]

[*Lady enters as gentleman makes last remark.*]

L.—Please show me your calicoes.

M. [*placing goods before her*]—Here are some very stylish patterns.

L.—Are they imported? [*examines.*]

M.—Just arrived this morning.

L.—This pattern is very pretty; what's the price?

M.—Seven and a half cents.

L.—Will the calico wash well?

M.—Madame, I'll warrant any of these [*taking hold of the calico*] to wash until there isn't a bit of color left in them.

L.—Indeed! I'll take ten yards.

M. [*measuring it*]—Shall I send it up?

L.—Yes; to 27 Broadway, seventh flat. [*Exit.*]

[*While the merchant is measuring, a second lady enters and looks at the goods on the table.*]

M.—What do you wish, Lady?

L.—How much are these sateens? [*holding up the goods.*]

M.—Five and a half cents to-day.

L.—That's too dear!

M.—Dear! You can't buy them elsewhere for less than five and three quarters. Here are some at four and a half. [*shows others.*]

12

L.—What horrid patterns!   Can't I have this one at the same price? [*holds up first.*]

M.—Can't afford it.

L.—I'll give you five cents.

M. [*shakes his head, no.*]

L.—You certainly will sell it for five and a quarter?

M.—I cannot change the price.

L. [*tossing the goods aside*]—Then I won't buy.

[*Exit.   Enter second gentleman, reading sign.*]

G.—" Bargains to-day."   Hope it's true.

M.—What can I show you?

G.—Toys.

M. [*holding articles up as he names them*]—Hoops, balls, dolls, ropes, anything you wish, sir.

G.—What's the price of a Noah's ark?

M. [*rubbing his head and looking around*]—Noah's ark? H'm.   We are just out of them.   Ordered some of Noah this morning.   [*Exit.*]   —*Helen W. Boyden.*

JUNE.

Sunbeams dancing with the daisies,
   South wind swinging in the grasses,
Butterflies' bewildering mazes,
     Gentle croon,
Where the dimpled brooklet passes,—
     This is June.

Insects humming in the meadow,
   Azure haze where vision closes,
Cloudless light, alluring shadow;
     Dreamy noon.
Filled with scent of hay and roses,—
     This is June.

SUCCESS.

The talent of success is nothing more than doing what you can well, without thought of fame.   —*Longfellow.*

VIOLETS.

Under the green hedges after the snow,
There do the dear little violets grow,
Hiding their modest and beautiful heads
Under the hawthorn, in soft mossy beds.

Sweet as the roses, and blue as the sky,
There do the dear little violets lie;
Hiding their heads where they scarce may be seen.
By the leaves you may know where the violet hath been.
                                   —*J. Moultrie.*

A TALE OF TWO BUCKETS.

Two buckets, in an ancient well, were talking once together,
And after sundry wise remarks, no doubt about the weather,
"Look here," quoth one, " this life we lead I don't exactly
      like;
Upon my word, I'm half inclined to venture on a strike;
For, do you mind? however full we both come up the well
We go down empty, always shall, for aught that I can tell."

"That's true," the other said; "but, then, the way it looks
      to me,
However empty we go down, we come up full, you see."
Wise little bucket! If we each would look at life that way,
'Twould dwarf its ills and magnify its blessings day by day:
The world would be a happier place, since we should all de-
      cide .
Only the buckets FULL to count and let the empty slide.
                                   —*Caroline E. Mason.*

NOWHERE.

Do you know where the summer blooms all the year round,
    Where there never is rain on a picnic day,
Where the thornless rose in its beauty grows,
    And the little boys never are called from play?
            Oh! hey! it is far away,
            In the wonderful land of Nowhere.

Would you like to live where nobody scolds,
　Where you never are told: " It's time for bed,"
Where you learn without trying, and laugh without crying,
　Where snarls never pull when they comb your head?
　　　　Then oh! hey! you must hie away
　　　　To the wonderful land of Nowhere.

If you long to dwell where you never need wait,
　Where no one is punished or made to cry,
Where a supper of cakes is not followed by aches,
　And little folks thrive on a diet of pie;
　　　　Then ho! hey! you must go, I say,
　　　　To the wonderful land of Nowhere.

You must drift down the river of Idle Dreams,
　Close to the border of No-man's land;
For a year and a day you must sail away,
　And then you will come to an unknown strand.
　　　　And ho! hey! if you get there—stay
　　　　In the wonderful land of Nowhere.

　　　　　　　　　　　　　　—*Ella Wheeler.*

THE WIND'S MISCHIEF.

　The wind was out for a frolic,
　　And a merry wight was he;
　With flying wing and whistling mouth
　Up he came from the far warm South,
　　To see what he could see.

　And he saw in Gold-Lock's garden
　　A full-blown apple-tree;
　And where the leaves were cosiest
　With leaf and blossom, he saw a nest,
　　As cunning as could be.

　And he paused in his mad-cap flying,
　　And murmured roguishly;
　" Oh, what will happen to that bird-house
　If I toss, and tumble, and shake the boughs?
　　I'll do it, just to see!"

So he caught the blossomed branches,
    And shook with a wicked glee;
Shook and shook, again and again,
And down there sprinkled a rosy rain
    Out from the apple-tree.

But the birdlings in the bird's nest
    Slumbered so cosily
That the mother sung in words like these
" Oh, what a loving, beautiful breeze
    To rock my babies for me! "

LIVE IN THE PRESENT.

Happy the man, and happy he alone,
He who can call to-day his own;
He who, secure within, can say,—
To-morrow do thy worst, for I have lived to-day.
        —*John Dryden.*

LITTLE JACK FROST.

Little Jack Frost went up the hill,
Watching the stars so cold and still;
Watching the stars and moon so bright,
And laughing aloud with all his might.
Little Jack Frost ran down the hill,
Late in the night when the winds were still;
Late in the fall when the leaves fell down,
Red and yellow and golden brown.

Little Jack Frost walked thro' the trees,
" Ah! " sighed the flowers, " We freeze! we freeze! "
" Ah! " sighed the grasses, " We die! we die! "
Said Little Jack Frost, " Good-bye! good-bye! "
Little Jack Frost tripped round and round,
Spreading white frost on the frozen ground,
Nipping the breezes, icing the streams,
Chilling the warmth of the sun's bright beams.

But when Dame Nature brought back the Spring,
Brought back the birds to chirp and sing,
Melted the snow and warmed the sky,
Then little Jack Frost went weeping by.
Flowers opened their eyes of blue,
Green buds peeped out and grasses grew,
And the sun beams warm shone o'er him so
That little Jack Frost was glad to go.

—Home, School and Nation.

THE SUM OF IT ALL.

The boy that by addition grows,
    And suffers no subtraction,
Who multiplies the things he knows,
    And carries every fraction,
Who well divides his precious time,
    The due proportion giving,
To sure success aloft will climb,
    Interest compound receiving.

—Dr. Ray Palmer.

THE ROSE'S CUP.

Down in a garden olden—
Just where I do not know—
A buttercup all golden
Chanced near a rose to grow.
And every morning early,
Before the birds were up,
A dozen dew-drops pearly
Fell in the golden cup.

This was the drink of water
The rose had every day,
But no one ever caught her
While drinking it, they say.
O, Rose, forgive the treason;
I say you drink so yet,
And that is just the reason
Your lips with dew are wet.

Harper's Young People.   *—Frank Dempster Sherman.*

PROVERBIAL WISDOM.

[Require the pupils to speak very distinctly and deliberately.]

First Pupil—We may be as good as we please, if we but please to be good.

Second Pupil—It is never too late to learn. One to-day is worth two to-morrows.

Third Pupil—Where there is a will there is a way. Lazy folks take the most pains.

Fourth Pupil—Labor conquers all. Step by step one goes a long way.

Fifth Pupil—Wealth may seek us, but wisdom must be sought.

Sixth Pupil—No one lives for himself alone. Always begin and end with God.

ONLY A FLOWER.

"Only a flower," the rich man said,
When he trod it down in his careless walk;
But his little daughter raised its head,
And tenderly held the broken stalk.

And from its place by the dusty way,
She carried it home to her garden small,
And set it where, from day to day,
Sunlight and shadow would on it fall.

It lived and thrived in the garden fair;
And when the autumn winds were chill,
And the roses died in the frosty air,
The hardy wild flower blossomed still.

The little maiden often smiled
To see it bloom when the rose was dead;
And the father, watching his happy child,
This sermon short in the blossom read:

Too often we crush with our careless feet
The flowers of love in our paths that blow,
And that cherished, would open full and sweet
When summer blossoms were lying low.

OUR PRINCIPLES.

First Boy—

Do our best, and leave the rest,
And never give up our trying.

Second Boy—

Be thoughtful for others;
Be sure and do right.
Be gentle and loving;
Be kind and polite.

Third Boy—

Dare to be brave in the cause of the right;
Dare with the enemy ever to fight,
Dare to be patient and loving each day;
Dare speak the truth whatever you say.

Fourth Boy—

Work for some good, be it ever so slowly,
Cherish some flower, be it ever so lowly,
Labor, all labor, is noble and holy!

GOOD ADVICE.

The man is sure to fall at last
Who does not stand alone;
Don't trust to other people's eyes,
But learn to mind your own.   —*John G. Saxe.*

THE CLOUD.

I bring fresh showers for the thirsting flowers
From the seas and the streams;
I bear light shades for the leaves when laid
In their noonday dreams.

From my wings are shaken the dews that waken
  The sweet buds every one,
When rocked to rest on their mother's breast,
  As she dances about the sun.
I wield the flail of the lashing hail,
  And whiten the green plains under,
And then again I dissolve it in rain,
  And laugh as I pass in thunder.

                    —Shelley.

THE BEST WE CAN.

When things don't go to suit us,
  Why should we fold our hands,
And say, " No use in trying,
  Fate baffles all our plans."
Let not your courage falter,
  Keep faith in God and man,
And to this thought be steadfast—
  "I'll do the best I can."

                    —E. E. Rexford.

NO ROYAL ROAD.

Is learning your ambition?
  There is no royal road;
Alike the peer and peasant
  Must climb to her abode;
Who feels the thirst of knowledge,
  In Helicon may slake it,
If he has still the Roman will
  To find a way, or make it.

                    —John G. Saxe.

THE AMERICAN BOY'S FUTURE.

In this glorious country, any American boy, however poor he may be, if he have a clear head, a true heart, and a strong arm, may rise through all grades of society, and become the crown, the glory, the pillar of the state.—*James A. Garfield.*

CLOSING PIECE.

So, then, our last words shall be for the Union. The
Union will guard the fame of its defenders, will keep alive for
mankind the beacon-lights of popular liberty and power; and
its mighty heart will throb with delight at every true advance
in any part of the world towards republican happiness and
freedom. —*George Bancroft.*

WHAT THE WINDS BRING.

Freddy—
> Which is the wind that brings the cold?

Large Girl—
> The North wind, Freddy, and all the snow;
> And the sheep will scamper into the fold
> When the North begins to blow.

Katie—
> Which is the wind that brings the heat?

Large Girl—
> The South wind, Katie; and corn will grow,
> And peaches redden for you to eat,
> When the South begins to blow.

Arty—
> Which is the wind that brings the rain?

Large Girl—
> The East wind, Arty; and farmers know
> That cows come shivering up the lane
> When the East begins to blow.

Bessie—
> Which is the wind that brings the flowers?

Large Girl—
> The West wind, Bessie; and soft and low
> The birdies sing in the summer hours
> When the West begins to blow.   —*E. C. Stedman.*

FOUR YEARS OLD.

What makes it night?   I want to go
Way off behind the sky and see.
The world's as round as it can be,
Somebody told me, so I know.

You yellow Moon, how bright you are!
Have all the stars been put to bed?
And is it true, as Nursey said,
That you're the baby stars' mamma?

And are they sometimes naughty too?
I cried a little bit to-day;
The tears would come,—where do they stay
When people's eyes won't let them thro'?

My dolly's in the grass out there,
Be quiet, Wind! you rustle so,
I'm 'fraid you'll wake her up, you know.
Please hush, dear Wind.   I wonder where

That four leaved clover is that grew
Down by the fence this afternoon.
I'm four years old, too.   Tell me, Moon,
When shall I be as old as you?

The clocks are striking in the town.
O, dear! I haven't said my prayers,
The little birds, I think, sing theirs,
I heard them when the sun went down.
—*Margaret Johnson.*

OUR DUTY.

Be you to others kind and true,
As you'd have others be to you;
And neither do nor say to men
Whate'er you would not take again.   —*Watts.*

CONTENTMENT.

A rich man, whatever his lot,
Is he who is content with what he's **got.**

WHAT WE MUST REMEMBER.

First Boy—

He is a coward who will not turn back
When first he discovers he's on the wrong track.

Second Boy—

It is as easy to draw back a stone, thrown with force from the hand, as to recall a word once spoken. —*Menander.*

Third Boy—

The way to gain a good reputation, is to endeavor to be what you desire to appear. —*Socrates.*

Fourth Boy—

The noblest courage is the courage to do right. —*Livy.*

LOST—THREE LITTLE ROBINS.

O, where is the boy, dressed in jacket of gray,
Who climbed up a tree in the orchard to-day,
And carried my three little birdies away?
    They hardly were dressed,
    When he took from the nest
My three little robins, and left me bereft.

O, wrens! have you seen, in your travels to-day,
A very small boy, dressed in jacket of gray,
Who carried my three little robins away?
    He had light-colored hair,
    And his feet were both bare,
Ah me! he was cruel and mean, I declare.

O, butterfly! stop just one moment, I pray;
Have you seen a boy dressed in jacket of gray,
Who carried my three little birdies away?
    He had pretty blue eyes,
    And was small of his size.
Ah! he must be wicked, and not very wise.

O, bees! with your bags of sweet nectarine, stay;
Have you seen a boy dressed in jacket of gray,
And carrying three little birdies away?
> Did he go through the town,
> Or go sneakin' aroun'
Through hedges and byways, with head hanging down?

O, boy with blue eyes, dressed in jacket of gray!
If you will bring back my three robins to-day,
With sweetest of music the gift I'll repay;
> I'll sing all day long
> My merriest song,
And I will forgive you this terrible wrong.

Bobolinks! did you see my birdies and me—
How happy we were on the old apple-tree—
Until I was robbed of my young, as you see?
> O, how can I sing,
> Unless he will bring
My three robins back, to sleep under my wing?

Songs for Our Darlings.   *—Aunt Clara.*

ALL FOR THE BEST.

Whichever way the wind doth blow,
Some heart is glad to have it so;
Then blow it east or blow it west,
The wind that blows, that wind is best.

REMEMBER THIS.

Sloth makes all things difficult; but Industry all easy;
and he that rises late must trot all day, but shall scarce over-
take his business at night; while Laziness travels so slowly
that Poverty soon overtakes him.   *—Franklin.*

CULTURE.

Men are polished, thro' act and speech,
> Each by each,
As pebbles are smoothed on the rolling beach.
      —J. T. Trowbridge.

EVENING IN WINTER.

(For Concert Recitation.)

Robed like an abbess
The snowy earth lies,
While the red sundown
Fades out of the skies.
Up walks the evening
Veiled like a nun,
Telling her starry beads,
One by one.

Where like the billows
The shadowy hills lie,
Like a mast the great pine swings
Against the bright sky.
Down in the valley
The distant lights quiver,
Gilding the hard-frozen
Face of the river.

When o'er the hilltops
The moon pours her ray,
Like shadows the skaters
Skirr wildly away;
Whirling and gliding
Like summer cloud fleet,
They flash the white lightning
From glittering feet.

The icicles hang
On the front of the falls,
Like mute horns of silver
On shadowy walls;
Horns that the wild huntsman
Spring shall awake,
Down flinging the loud blast
Toward river and lake!   —*T. B. Read.*

JOHNNY ON GRANDMOTHERS.

I'm sure I can't see at all
　　What a poor fellow ever could do
For apples, and pennies and cake,
　　Without a grandmother or two.

And if he is bad now and then,
　　And makes a great racketing noise,
They only look over their specs,
　　And say, "Ah, these boys will be boys!

" Life is only so short at the best;
　　Let the children be happy to-day."
Then they look for a while at the sky,
　　And the hills that are far, far away.

Quite often, as twilight comes on,
　　Grandmothers sing hymns very low
To themselves, as they rock by the fire,
　　About heaven and when they shall go.

And then, a boy stopping to think,
　　Will find a hot tear in his eye,
To know what will come at the last;
　　For grandmothers all have to die.

I wish they could stay here and pray,
　　For a boy needs their prayers every night,
Some boys more than others, I 'spose;
　　Such as I need a wonderful sight.

———

THE SUMMER SHOWER.
(*For Concert Recitation.*)

Before the stout harvesters falleth the grain,
As when the strong storm wind is reaping the plain
And loiters the boy in the briery lane;
But yonder aslant comes the silvery rain,
Like a long line of spears, burnished and tall.

Adown the white highway, like cavalry fleet,
It dashes the dust with its numberless feet.
Like a murmurless school in their leafy retreat,
The wild birds sit listening, the drops round them beat.
And the boy crouches close to the blackberry wall.
The swallows alone take the storm on their wing,
And, taunting the tree-sheltered laborers, sing.
Like pebbles the rain breaks the face of the spring,
While a bubble darts up from each widening ring;
And the boy, in dismay, hears the loud shower fall.

But soon are the harvesters tossing the sheaves;
The robin darts out from its bower of leaves;
The wren peereth forth from the moss-covered eaves;
And the rain-spattered urchin now gladly perceives
That the beautiful bow bendeth over them all.

—T. Buchanan Read.

LOVE EVERYWHERE.

God scatters love on every side
Freely among his children all,
And always hearts are lying open wide,
Wherein some grains may fall.

—J. R. Lowell.

THE SWEET SONG.

This world is full of beauty, like other worlds above,
And if we did our duty it might be full of love.

—Gerald Massey.

WISE WORDS.

First Pupil—A good name is rather to be chosen than great riches, and loving favor rather than silver and gold.

Second Pupil—A soft answer turneth away wrath, but grievous words stir up anger.

Third Pupil—Withhold not good from them to whom it is due, when it is in the power of thine hand to do it.

—Solomon.

www.ingramcontent.com/pod-product-compliance
Lightning Source LLC
Chambersburg PA
CBHW030839270326
41928CB00007B/1134